Collards

Collards

A Southern Tradition from Seed to Table

EDWARD H. DAVIS
& JOHN T. MORGAN

The University of Alabama Press

Tuscaloosa

The University of Alabama Press
Tuscaloosa, Alabama 35487-0380
uapress.ua.edu

Publication supported in part by Emory and Henry College,
Emory, Virginia
Inquiries about reproducing material from this work should
be addressed to the University of Alabama Press.

Typeface: Scala Pro

Manufactured in the United States of America
Cover photograph: Freshly picked collards for sale
at the Carrboro, North Carolina, Farmers' Market.
Photo courtesy of Bradley A. Crittenden
Author photograph: (*left to right*) Edward H. Davis
and John T. Morgan; courtesy of Brent Treash,
Emory & Henry College Public Relations
Cover and interior design: Michele Myatt Quinn

∞

The paper on which this book is printed meets the
minimum requirements of American National Standard for
Information Sciences—Permanence of Paper for Printed
Library Materials, ANSI Z39.48-1984.

Library of Congress Cataloging-in-Publication Data

Davis, Edward H.
Collards: a southern tradition from seed to table /
Edward H. Davis and John T. Morgan.
pages cm
Includes bibliographical references and index.
ISBN 978-0-8173-1834-5 (cloth: alk. paper) —
ISBN 978-0-8173-8765-5 (e book)
1. Collards. I. Morgan, John (John T.) II. Title.
SB351.K3D38   2015
635'.347—dc23   2014030647

Contents

CONTENTS

Tables

Preface

"Isn't the collard plant just a weed?" We have heard that question many times, usually from some poor soul deprived of all southern culture. How tragic a mistake, to reduce to the status of a primitive pest a living organism that evolved over centuries of cultural development, lifetimes of cultivation and care, and periodic moments of culinary genius. As geographers who know something of the glory of collards, we are compelled to repair the error—and, thus, to write this book.

Contemporary Southerners owe much to the collard lovers who came before us—the cooks who developed and passed down over centuries so many delectable ways to prepare collards. We also owe thanks to those pioneers of the garden who did the work to develop the collard plant to what we know today. They were the unheralded gardeners and farmers who took the less tasty, even unpalatable plants they found growing wild and gradually improved them by amateur breeding. This domestication occurred over generations, beginning thousands of years ago. It was done primarily by the saving of seed, a skill now confined largely to a shrinking number of botanists and a scattering of unique hobbyists. Until the nineteenth century, however, it was standard practice in all rural places. This book must, therefore, go across the Atlantic to the sources of a rural landscape.

Imagine this: In the early 1700s, in a village somewhere in England, a woman slipped a spoonful of collard seed into a cloth bag. Not long afterward she left her home and boarded a ship for Charleston, in the American colonies. After she arrived, she began to plant her garden. She also had brought seeds for such favorites as carrots, turnips, and peas, but she knew the collard seed would be particularly helpful, for it would produce plants unlike any other vegetable in their ability to nourish.

Most importantly, the collard would produce a large number of supremely nutritious leaves that she would cut and boil to serve as greens. Several other plants—such as cabbage, dandelion, and spinach—served this same purpose, but the collard offered something more: Even after summer was over, each plant would continue to produce new leaves throughout the fall and winter and into early spring. So a small plot of perhaps twenty-five collard plants could provide a family of four with weekly or twice-weekly greens for up to ten months. This abundance is why our English migrant called this plant "cut-and-come-again."

She made a small label for her seed bag that read "colewort," which is the Old English word for cole plant (the cole or *Brassica* family includes what we know as collards, as well as cabbage and kale). Her pronunciation had shifted to the easier "collard," and over the next hundred years the spelling would gradually follow suit. Although by the 1830s people who stayed in England had largely forgotten the collard and adopted in its place the heading form—cabbage—for reasons we'll get to later, in the Southern colonies, the collard had become a standard feature of the fall and winter landscape as well as diet and remained so for nearly two centuries.

Our English gardener is hypothetical, for there is no specific record of an immigrant bringing collard seed to the American colonies. We are talking about a pre-commercial act, carried out thousands of times as people came from England, Wales, Scotland, and Ireland at a time when most garden seed was simply saved and passed between generations. The ship manifests of those days and the diaries of educated and wealthier travelers often included lists of seeds but specified only those for cash crops, such as barley or wheat. All kinds of European vegetable seeds were brought over but were only listed as "garden seed." So the entry (actually multiple entries) of collards to America passed without documentation. Perhaps the men who prepared such documents neglected such details because the kitchen garden was considered merely women's domestic work.

Even less likely to be recorded in early American history were the millions of times that collards were cooked. Again, that was woman's work and not a commodity; hence, these acts were ignored by those with pen and paper. But with considerable skill and creativity—and without written recipes—African American women (and sometimes even men) turned collards into a Southern delight.

Evidence suggests that collards eaten by colonists had only some beef fat or ham hock added during cooking for flavor, which perhaps explains reports that green vegetables were unpopular in early British America. Still, through the 1800s, over much of the South, collards were a common, even a standard, table item. How did that happen?

African American cooks deserve the lead credit for the diffusion of collards across the South. These often uneducated women and men carried in their ancient cultural wisdom two important notions: dark leafy greens are essential to our health, and proper proportions of peppers and other spices make cooked vegetables taste much better. So the collard, a rather minor player in British cuisine, would become a major one in the American South because of African culinary and nutritional wisdom.[1] Exactly how that happened may have fallen between the cracks in the historical record, but in this work we have collected glimpses of the collard's remarkable story from over two centuries and across ten states. Today, outside the South, the green is still barely known, and even most Southern children find enjoying collards requires repeated efforts, yet this food clearly has the gumption to stay with us. This book is about that gumption—how a simple plant, properly grown and cooked, holds the power to find approbation from millions of Southern palates.

We boldly conjecture that a forkful of collards contains more Southern history than any other bite. This simple food was eaten widely in the Southern colonies by the time of the American Revolution, and its place in the region's cuisine has been gradually strengthened in the following two centuries. Collards have been appreciated by some of the greatest Southerners, from Thomas Jefferson to Martin Luther King Jr., and yet have also sustained some of the region's most marginalized people. You could say the same about cornbread, fried chicken, barbeque, fried green tomatoes, grits, sweet tea, or okra; these are also classically Southern—as the wonderful people at the Southern Foodways Alliance in Oxford, Mississippi, can tell you—but those foods have been widely adopted beyond the South.[2] The flavor of collards is uniquely Southern, which may explain why few Americans living outside the South—other than "expatriates"—have made collards a part of their culture. *The New Encyclopedia of Southern Culture, Volume 7*, edited by John T. Edge, the renowned food expert and director of the Southern Foodways Alliance, even claims that collards, "probably more than any other food, delineate the boundaries of the Mason-Dixon line."[3] If for no other reason, such a claim indicates that collards deserve a closer look.

Although collards may not have found much favor among most non-Southern Americans, they are linked to the very core historical facts of the American South, in the confluence of African and British folkways. Collard seed was deliberately transported from the gardens of ordinary British people. On the other hand, Africans—who were not allowed to carry a thing when transported to this country—nonetheless brought an asset just as essential: their culinary knowledge, which included an understanding of, and preference for, dark leafy greens. That knowledge, and the food tradition that built on it among blacks and whites alike, no doubt saved many Southerners from starvation.

Contemplate the fact that a forkful of collards has, ounce for ounce, more nutritional value than nearly any other green vegetable, with only spinach having more nutrients. Southerners, black and white, have intentionally sustained a very wise cultural trait in their preference for this food, in spite of considerable derision from outsiders—and even a few insiders. No other Southern food, with the possible exception of chitterlings and pork rinds, has had to persist under such ridicule. Collards may not be spreading beyond the South like the less healthful pecan pie, sweet tea, and banana pudding, but they have certainly played a role in nutritional eating.

Because of its importance as a food staple, the collard has been commonly grown in "collard patches," visible in the fall and winter landscape in parts of the South for over 200 years. These patches may have as few as five plants or upwards of fifty, but usually contain at least fifteen. The collard plant, known scientifically as *Brassica oleracea*, var. *acephala*, is sometimes called a headless cabbage. (As we shall see later, it would be more appropriate to call cabbage a heading collard.) The collard is indeed closely related to cabbage, but in the South the former has two advantages over the latter: it is better able to endure hot summers, while thriving as well as cabbage in winter; and collard greens are richer than cabbage (and nearly any other vegetable) in Vitamin A, additionally providing significant amounts of Vitamin C, calcium, and iron. Taken together, these assets mean the collard is a blessing to the South.

A book about any Southern food will necessarily reflect on tangled Southern interfaces—the conflicts of race, class, and gender that have always moved and shaken the region and its cultural practices. For example, many Southern foods result from the mingling of West African, Native American, and European ingredients and cooking methods. Tomatoes were a Native American food, but they became a leading Southern ingredient after they were breaded and fried while still green, or sliced and served on bread with mayonnaise. Okra was domesticated in Africa, where it was cooked in stews, but became a classic Southern food once it was breaded and fried in a skillet. And when Southerners prepare a "mess" of collards, they are stirring up European and African traditions.

Covering as much of the region as possible, this book reflects a "greens culture" permeating the Southern landscape, written by two geographers who set about stalking the Southern collard. We believe it is the first cultural, social, and historical geography of this important regional food and crop. Toward that purpose, we explore the iconic status of collards in popular culture; describe the traditions of growing the crop, as well as cooking and eating collard greens; seek to determine the origin and pattern of diffusion of collards to the South; trace the development of the food crop through time; delineate the geography of collard production in the South; and describe and assess the changing status of the plant in the region.

Our discussion and conclusions are based largely on field work conducted throughout the South over the past decade. In the research process we recorded the presence of collard patches and fields; surveyed agricultural extension agents, college students, and other informed people; and interviewed hundreds of people whose lives connect to collards, such as gardeners, farmers, scientists, wholesalers, seed retailers, grocery store managers, and restaurant cooks and managers. We drove the back roads of more than half of the 888 counties in our study area to seek out those informants and to observe and record wide varieties of home gardens and commercial fields (see fig. 3). In addition, we consulted primary historical documents and census data. We also visited Britain, Portugal, and Ghana to seek the origins of the American collard. Based on a collation of the work of botanists, garden historians, and plant taxonomists, and of our own mapping of primary documents, we have developed a theory of how and where collards entered colonial America and how they became widespread throughout the South.

We chose to focus our studies on ten Southern states (in geographic order from west to east): Arkansas, Louisiana, Mississippi, Tennessee, Alabama, Florida, Georgia, South Carolina, North Carolina, and Virginia. Beyond those states, greens are relatively less popular, and collards are rare. For example, although Kentucky has some restaurants serving collards, the number of collard gardeners seems to be insignificant, and greens in general seem to be less popular than they are in other southern states.

Now, do as your mother admonished and eat your greens!

Acknowledgments

We'd like to thank our wives, Sandy Davis and Sally Morgan, for their patience and constant support; our mothers, Lucy Davis and Annie Morgan, for loving us and cooking such good food; Whit Davis for his field work assistance and excellent backseat driving; Leslie Lloyd, Lisa Eskridge, and Karin Widener for their wonderful office help; Jane Caldwell for her library research help; Beth Motherwell, our editor at the University of Alabama Press, for all her support; Professors John Fraser Hart and Wilbur Zelinsky for their encouragement of this project; Mark Farnham for help with the genetics and the seed saver project; Wesley Greene at Colonial Williamsburg for his help with garden history; Powell Smith for help with commercial collards and pest management; Bobby Wilson for his help in Atlanta; Professor Antonio Monteiro for his help in Portugal; Professors Sosthenes Kufogbe and Carol Markwei for their help on West African greens; Michael Quinion for help with the etymology of *collard*; Freda Butner, Registered Dietician, for help on nutrition; Cheryl Lange and Stan Cope at Bonnie Plants for their sales data; Michael Roberts, Mary Cheatham, Ella Woods, Reanell Bradley, and Stacy Gaskins for sharing their recipes; Hoyt Taylor, Professor Steven Hopp, and several anonymous readers for helpful suggestions on the manuscript; and all the many faculty members at two- and four-year institutions across the South who distributed and collected student food and garden surveys.

Collards

1

Celebrating Collards

From Festivals to Fiction

SOUTHERN FESTIVALS

IT'S AYDEN, NORTH CAROLINA, on the first weekend in September, and the aroma of good cooking tantalizes the sense of smell. Everything called "comfort food" is available from the various vendors: local-style barbeque, cole slaw, ham biscuits, fried chicken, funnel cakes, ice cream, macaroni and cheese, and fried pies. But this is the Ayden Collard Festival, where the celebrant is collards. And brave attendees can sign up for the annual—and probably the world's only—collard-eating contest.

Contestants are given a fork and a chair at the table on the town's main stage, where they are offered a series of one-pound servings of collards. They have precisely thirty minutes to eat as many pounds of collards as possible, and for a full five minutes after the 30-minute bell sounds and eating has ended, contestants must avoid regurgitating all those pounds of collards. Apparently quite a few contestants fail this last requirement. To help "grease the skids," hot pepper sauce may be used to flavor the collards, and cups of water are offered to contestants. Judges watch closely, as does the audience, knowing that someone just might try to hide a few fork-loads up a sleeve, down a shirt, or off the back of the stage.

The current record is a fantastic *eight and a quarter pounds*, set by an out-of-towner named Willy Holden in 2004. The previous record-holder, Mort Hurst of nearby Robertsonville, North Carolina, ate seven and a half pounds in the 1984 contest. Hurst was proud of having held the record for twenty years and still finds it hard to believe his long-standing record was legitimately beaten. That's why he was on the stage as a kind of unauthorized judge during the 2005 contest. Hurst was back in town after years of absence; he had stopped entering or even observing, confident that his record would never be broken. He is, in fact, a contender in many different eating contests at other festivals and takes his vocation seriously. This time, he was in Ayden to see the new record-holder at work; Hurst was watching for signs of greatness—or fraud.

The 2005 Collard Eating Contest began with sixteen contestants, watched closely by the judges as the participants trudged their way through pound after pound of collards. Each new one-pound container was delivered by the young beauty queens who had been awarded the title of "Collard Queen" in various age categories (see fig. 2).

Some contestants left the stage at the fifteen minute mark, having eaten too much too quickly. By the twenty-minute mark, only eight contestants were still on stage, slogging through forkful after forkful, most using sips of water to ease the influx down their throats. By the twenty-five minute mark, the women's category winner was clear—Mary Dennison, age 30, was the only woman left on stage.

After several departures, the default winner in the male category was Harold Smith, age 63, of Pink Hill, North Carolina, who had eaten only four and a half pounds but was able to hold it down afterward. Smith had won in two previous years, so maybe that explains his quiet demeanor just after the victory. As he strolled through the admiring festival crowd, he did comment that he needed to lie down.

But in the minutes just after the contest, Harold was proud to be photographed with the women's titleholder. Dennison was born and raised up north and said she had never heard of collards until she moved to Greenville, North Carolina two years ago. Now she loves them, especially those served at Bum's Restaurant. Dennison and Smith each won a ribbon and $100 cash, but they immediately took their prize money over to the Red Cross booth and donated it toward the Hurricane Katrina relief campaign.

The Ayden Collard Festival draws between seven and ten thousand visitors each year, attracted by the food, live music, stage shows, amusement rides, parade complete with beauty queens of all ages, and a 5K race that benefits Habitat for Humanity. For more than thirty years, the organizers have followed a key strategy for creating a good community festival: focus on local foods. The food vendors are the most successful operators at this festival, especially those selling comfort foods high in fat, sugar, or carbohydrates—or all three. Nevertheless, collards sell well at this festival (at least two thousand servings each year), and the community is proud to be associated with this traditional food. All the festival's popular hats and T-shirts are designed to prominently show a collard plant, usually as a comical character. And none of the beauty queens seem at all embarrassed to be called a Collard Queen.

The friendly threshold of Bum's Restaurant (open since 1963, owned by Latham "Bum" Dennis) sits at the very center of Ayden, right where the old bank building looks down on the railroad crossing. This is where patrons enjoy classic eastern North Carolina barbeque, which comes with cornbread and a side of Bum's collards (see fig. 5).

Bum is a hardworking man who has figured out how to draw customers from country and city alike with his down-home food and outgoing personality. Bum's flavorful barbeque is made from roughly chopped pork in a vinegar sauce, the kind of barbeque for which eastern North Carolina is famous. But his cooked collards are a departure from the variety most Carolinians like, a regional favorite called "cabbage collard" or "yellow cabbage collard," which is milder than the more common collard type and even said to be sweeter. What Bum cooks with is a darker, stronger collard—in fact, he sells a collard like no other, since he grows his own collards from seed that has been saved over generations—lately by him—in a large garden that he maintains just for his restaurant.

Being particular has paid off, for Bum's collards are featured in the eating contest held in Ayden's annual festival. His greens are so famous that Bum bristles at the phrase *side dish*. "They're not a *side dish*. They're what I would call a *feature*."

One of the past winners of the Collard Queen contest, Stacy Gaskins—a young woman born and raised in Ayden—is now the director of the Ayden Chamber of Commerce. She says that most people she knows have at least a small collard patch and that one of her wedding gifts was a *collard pot*. Similar to a large stock pot, it is named for its local standard use. "I also got a collard chopper," she said. "It's just a kind of circular blade with a handle that makes it easier to chop collards than by using knives."

An act designed to celebrate collards can be the result of bold boosterism. Such is the case for Conecuh County, Alabama, which is the state's "collard green capital," an honor unknown even to most citizens of Alabama. This designation dates to legal action in 1998: "Be it resolved by the House of Representatives of the Legislature of Alabama, that Conecuh County is hereby designated as Collard Green Capital of Alabama, and that the proper officials are hereby authorized to erect appropriate signs and markers."[1] Local boosters, led by Luther Upton from radio station WPPG, had organized the first annual Collard Festival in the county seat of Evergreen and sought the designation as a way to bring tourists to town. The festival ran for about four years and may be defunct now.

Successful town festivals are usually dependent on a small group of tough, committed women. Another of the South's small collard festivals lasted a little over a decade in the tiny crossroads of Ponce de Leon, Florida, which has a population of only four hundred. Millions of drivers pass through the area as they whip through Holmes County on Interstate 10, just half a mile to the south. The Homemakers' Club of Ponce de Leon held a collard festival in this tiny Panhandle town on the Saturday after Thanksgiving from 1980 to 1991.

Local resident Phyllis Lake, along with several friends, took care of the innumerable details involved in feeding thousands of people in one spot and on a single day, all to raise money for the local chapter of the American Cancer Society. "That first year we called it a 'fall dinner,' and we set up to serve food in the city hall. We had a nice kitchen at our disposal, so it seemed like a good little scheme. We had hoped about 200 people would come out, but we got 600 that first year, and we knew we had found something that worked. We knew we could make pretty good money if we had enough food to sell, so we decided to move to the high school cafeteria the next year and call it a Collard Festival. Then it was so much bigger than we ever figured."

Lake described the plan: "We got a local farmer, Henry Padgett, to plant a large field of collards just for us. We put notices in the papers, we ordered T-shirts and hats, we found judges for the collard queen beauty contest, and we signed up musicians to play country or gospel music. We asked important community people to be our judges for the collard-cooking contest. We ordered about twenty-five big cured hams from a local meat packer. I would start about a month ahead of time preparing the crackling bread. I would buy corn meal and hog fat, cook it up, and make the corn pones and store them in the freezer. We baked them in the cafeteria during the festival so they were fresh.

"Just before the festival our volunteers would go to Mr. Padgett's farm to crop the collards. We'd lay out big sheets and pile the collard leaves on them. Then we would cut off the stems and break the leaves. We'd bring them to the school to wash them in big tubs and chop them up. To cook the collards we had to use twenty-two 8-gallon stock pots. And they were full. We'd sell about forty-four pots of collards every year."

The festival petered out after 1991, she says, partly because the women who took over the kitchen decided the collards and other foods needed to be fat free and sugar free. "That was the end, because people were coming out to have a special dinner. They didn't come out for health food. So a whole lot of food didn't get eaten, and the organizers gave up." Lake lives alone, her husband having died some years ago, and continues to keep a garden. She offers a collard soup recipe from her late friend Mary Martin, who was an excellent cook. [2] That recipe can be found toward the end of Chapter Three.

LITERARY COLLARDS

When a regional food gets mentioned in a novel, it could be just a device to give the story some "local flavor." But William Faulkner spent his writing career shining a light on the society he knew so well from his hometown of Oxford, Mississippi. He seldom wrote about food, mentioning turnip greens only twice in his writings (in the short story "There Was a Queen" and in his novel *The Hamlet*). He wrote about collards just once: in a powerful passage from his 1948 short novel *Intruder in the Dust*, Faulkner describes a white Mississippi boy's reaction to the dinner food he shares in a black family's cabin as "collard greens, a slice of side meat fried in flour, big flat pale heavy half-cooked biscuits, a glass of buttermilk: nigger food too, accepted and then dismissed also because it was what they liked, what they chose: not (at twelve: he would be a man grown before he experienced his first amazed dubiety at this) that out of their long chronicle this was all they had had a chance to learn to like except the ones who ate out of white folk's kitchens but that they had elected this out of all eating because this was their palates and their metabolism."[3]

Faulkner is striking at one of the pillars of racism: the belief that the conditions faced by black people derive, in the words of historian Timothy Tyson, from "not our history but their genes."[4] Perhaps such misconceptions about foodways are still propped up by such racial prejudices. Some of the white people we interviewed in some parts of the South seemed surprised when they were asked if they liked collards. A few, trying not to offend, quietly intimated that "collards are black folk's food." Modern Oxford, Mississippi, however, gives no evidence of disgust for any greens: the local grocery stores sell plenty of collards, turnip greens, and mustard greens, to both black and white people, according to their produce managers.

Sometimes collards' supposed lack of sophistication inspires an author. In the Walker Percy story "The Last Donahue Show," published in 1983, a visitor from another planet shows up at the taping of an episode of *The Phil Donahue Show* where guests are debating the issue of sexual orientation. The visitor finds the debate incomprehensible. He informs those present that the end is near and the last refuge is a cave in Lost Cove, Tennessee. To make this cave a livable place, it has been stocked with sweet corn, grits, sausage, and collard greens. The visitor, identified by Percy simply as "the cosmic intruder," is performing the role of a doomsday prophet. But why do grits and collard greens find honor with this extraterrestrial prophet? Perhaps no other Southern foods remain truly vernacular, authentically plain. Perhaps Percy, who was raised in Greenville, Mississippi, chooses them because they are considered less commercialized and, therefore, not as corrupted as other modern foods.[5]

Along the same lines—the collard celebrated as down-to-earth—is the prayer spoken by a character in Clyde Edgerton's novel *Lunch at the Piccadilly*:

> O God in us all, may we embrace the rooms of refuge food. Real food, cheap food, food served by people with wet rags under their arms. . . . Oh, the dying and bygone potential union of blacks and rednecks . . . once a thread, food thread or not, always frazzled, a thread of religion and family habits and knowledge of geography, now frayed beyond repair and only redeemable through cabbage, collards, turnip salet, fried fatback, the slunken foods now reserved for movies and poverty . . . and selected sanitation-grade B cafeterias and some small farms and old evaporated dreams of slack-jawed beggars. Help us, O God in us all, help us reinvent, remember, the proper cooking of foods of the home, foods that feed our attitudes and make bonds where none will otherwise be, foods from the childhoods of old people that will bring to their hearts—through their mouths—precious memories . . . Make us ministers of memory.[6]

Edgerton was born in Durham, North Carolina.

Urban identity is tied to notions of sophistication that may lead people to be ashamed of collards eaten and enjoyed during their upbringing. The same might be assumed of the upper class in the South. However, in one popular portrayal of the nineteenth century's upper class—Margaret Mitchell's hugely successful novel *Gone with the Wind*, published in 1936— collards are celebrated, rather than derided.

Scarlett survives the Civil War only to find her family's plantation fallen into ruin. Her family and former slaves now depend on her, but there is barely enough food to sustain them. In the film version, this crisis is compressed into the sunset scene where in her desperate hunger she pulls up a turnip, takes a bite and experiences an epiphany: She has the inner resources to survive and thrive again. She lifts the turnip to the heavens and pronounces, "As God is my witness I'll never be hungry again." This is the scene moviegoers most recall, but the novel has a more extended garden scene in which Scarlett dreams about the wonderful meals of her pre-war life: "Rolls, corn muffins, biscuits and waffles, dripping butter, all at one meal. Ham at one end of the table and fried chicken at the other, collards swimming richly in pot liquor iridescent with grease, snap beans in mountains on brightly flowered porcelain, fried squash, stewed okra, carrots in cream sauce thick enough to cut. And three desserts, so everyone might have his choice, chocolate layer cake, vanilla blanc mange, and pound cake topped with sweet whipped cream."[7] Praising collards along with these other foods equates them in status, classifying them as foods not associated with poverty. In addition, Mitchell gives a strong impression that, at least in the 1930s, collards were not identified with only black or white Southerners.

These examples of collards mentioned—even celebrated—in American fiction, extend to poetry and song as well. Some American poets, such as Langston Hughes, Atsuro Riley, Fred Chappell, Nola Garrett, and Carl Hancock Rux, to name a few, have also intoned collards in their works.

Excerpt from "Florida" (1999) by poet Cornelius Eady:

> . . . while my parents' house might sit in Upstate
> New York, the truth of the matter is that we were raised in Florida.
> The smells rising from the skillets—Florida.

The car parts on the lawn—Florida.
The switch across the legs—Florida.

The fact was that we resided in the deep, black south, even when we were walking around in a blizzard, or sitting at a lunch counter without giving it a second thought.

The "dry" barbecue pit in the backyard—Florida.
The black cats and the ghosts—Florida.
The sunflowers in the front yard, and
The collard greens in the back—Florida.[8]

An excerpt from a poem published in 2005 by Atsuro Riley, born and raised in South Carolina:

Keen-pipit *Snap-Beans, Pot-Beans, Sweet-Potato-Shoes; Collard-Bills (in Hock-Stock), Hoppin' John—and Okra Stew. Cabbage Pie, Cymbling Fry, Crowder-Peas in Cream; Cornbread (Tea-Glassed, Buttermilked), Streak-of-Lean & Creasy Greens!*[9]

Poems about collards actually had their fifteen minutes of fame back in 1984, when a couple of North Carolina English professors, Luke Whisnant and Alex Albright, announced a collard poetry contest, news of which was picked up by some local newspapers and then the *Atlanta Constitution, USA Today*, and the Canadian Broadcasting Corporation. Ultimately, nearly five hundred submissions were received, from thirty-two states and Europe. Whisnant and Albright published a book *Leaves of Greens*, containing one hundred and twenty-seven of the submissions, including one called "The Monk is Deep" by renowned poet Fred Chappell:

You know who used to wear a collard in his lapel just like a proud carnation?

Thelonious Sphere Monk from North Carolina is who.

I like to imagine some hotstuff jazz critic
—maybe Leonard Feather or another jiveass—
Asking, Say Monk what *is* that thing you've got on?

        And Thelonious replies:
You looking at my sole credentials.[10]

Another poem published in *Leaves of Greens* was this poignant one by
Roger Swagler of Athens, Georgia, called "Mama, Fix Collard Greens for Me":

She sits in her flat on Manhattan's East Side
With her Chablis and French Camembert
While back in Pitt County, her sweet mother's tears
Wash the page as she writes in despair:

"It used to be 'Mama, fix collards for me,'
But now you're ashamed, yes it's true,
Of the mama which fed you . . ." her mother then stopped,
For she knew words alone would not do.

So clinging to hope she rushed out in her yard,
Cut her collards and added some pork.
Then she went to the phone and called Federal Express
And shipped the whole mess to New York.

The collards arrived and her daughter was sad
As she looked at them there on the plate.
For she'd hurt her dear mother, but just then a friend
Tried the greens and said, "Oh! These are great."

And now in New York you'll not find wine and cheese
At the clearly most fashionable scenes.
Oh, no, if you're upwardly mobile and hip,
The smart thing's to eat collard greens.

Collards are also included in song lyrics: an old-time song composed by South Georgia fiddler Warren Smith in the late 1940s was given the title "Rabbit under a Collard Leaf."[11] This song was common in primary schools during the 1930s in Wallace, on North Carolina's coastal plain:

> It's collard greens, it's collard greens.
> First thing you do, better put 'em in the pot;
> Next thing to do, you'd better eat 'em while it's hot;
> It's collard greens.[12]

A hit song called "Collard Greens and Cornbread" by R&B star Fantasia Barrino was released in 2010 on her Grammy-nominated album *Back to Me*. The song, composed by Nigerian singer-songwriter Tiwa Savage, has as its central lyric this line: "Even got the nerve to say, you're better than my mama's collard greens and cornbread." The song has considerable sexual innuendo, implying that home-cooked collards are so good that one *might* prefer eating them to making love.

COLLARD GREENS IN *SOUTHERN LIVING* MAGAZINE

Collard consumption is fairly high in the historic city of Birmingham, Alabama, where African Americans staged some of their early battles for freedom. This city is now the center of a major metropolitan area, where much has changed since the days of Jim Crow. Racial divides still exist, but the city's residents mingle now with less attention to skin color. The metro area has grown to a population of 1.2 million (2009 census estimate), about a quarter of the state's population. Hundreds of restaurants serve nearly every kind of food, and black and white folk share these spaces daily—many of them eating and enjoying collards.

Birmingham is more than just a large Southern city, however. It is the place where regional identity, indeed Southernness, is made incarnate— even molded—by one very successful project: *Southern Living* magazine. *Southern Living* currently has about three million subscribers, making it among the top twenty magazines nationwide, and is by far the most successful regional magazine in the country. *Sunset* magazine, which focuses on the American West, has fewer than half that many subscribers. Birmingham, therefore, hosts a major force in the shaping of both Southern food culture and the rest of the country's *perception* of the South.

When *Southern Living* was introduced in February 1966, its president, Eugene Butler, stated up front that his publication was "especially for urban and suburban people of the South."[13] Rural Southerners were clearly seen as a diminishing market, and the content of the magazine has reflected this bias ever since. Although articles on hunting, fishing, and camping, and advertisements for outboard motors, fishing gear, and shotgun shells appeared regularly, the magazine mainly targeted white women of the middle-class suburbs. Because it sought to present the "New South" to a national and even to an international audience, the editors were self-conscious about Southern identity.[14] History was glamorized to a high urban-tourist sheen, and rural traditions such as home vegetable gardening were seldom mentioned. The garden section preached perfect lawns, hybrid flowers, and flowering shrubs. *Southern Living*'s tastes were decidedly expensive, and the overall look was a blend of global fashion and "high-end rustic."

We did a complete search of each issue for representation of greens history. Scouring each monthly issue, which often contains some forty recipes, we found that cooked greens were not mentioned for the first three years of publication. For the creators of the magazine, southern "living" was done with other vegetables. A recipe for turnip greens with pot liquor, sent in by a subscriber from Houston, Texas, was included in April 1969. Then, in January 1971, an article appeared that must be considered a watershed. Titled "Southern Soul Food Goes Gourmet," the article declares: "Members of the jet set have a new 'thing' going in the food line. They have discovered soul food. Small eating places in many areas of the North specialize in those foods that have been popular in the South for years. Let's face it: greens, 'pot likker,' and corn pone have hit the big time. Southerners have known all along about fried salt pork and country ham, collard and turnip greens, black-eyed peas cooked with ham hock, cornbread, and sweet potato pie. Maybe it just took this latest kick of the gourmet set to make a hostess unself-conscious about serving friends a meal of this sort."[15]

The article is accompanied by a photo of several white people having great fun and clearly savoring their "soul" experience. The article includes recipes for black-eyed peas with ham hock, country cornbread, sweet potato pie, fried ham with red-eye gravy, and fresh greens.

Fresh Greens

¼ lb salt pork, diced
1 large bunch turnip, mustard, or collard greens
½ cup boiling water
Salt to taste

Cook the salt pork in the water 10 minutes, add washed greens, and cook until tender. Salt to taste. Don't overcook. Serve with vinegar.

This was a breakthrough for more down-home cooking. Over the next two decades, recipes for cooked greens would appear every few years. Since the seventies, *Southern Living* has become much more integrated and now regularly celebrates more rural Southern culture.

Since the early 1990s, collards recipes have been included in the magazine at least once a year. For almost twenty years now, the December or January issue will contain a collard recipe, usually with a paragraph about the "Southern tradition" of eating greens (whether turnip, collard, or mustard) with black-eyed peas on New Year's Day to bring good fortune. The higher profile given to collards rather than the other greens may result from recognition by the food editors that collards sell in larger amounts than other greens. On the other hand, the choice to highlight collards may come as a surprise to the millions of people who live in those parts of the South where turnip or mustard greens are more popular.

COLLARDS AND RACE

Complicating the conscious choice to highlight collards is the always am-
biguous nature of racial identity. More than any other food, collards have
become a symbol of African American cuisine, in spite of the fact that
many Southerners see collards as simply a "Southern" or "country" dish. It
seems that foodways may be artificially split even today along racial lines.
Having grown up unaware of any racial split in Southern food culture, only
now have the authors of this book come to see that collard culture must be
understood in light of African American identity.

As already noted, Thelonious Monk, the great jazz composer and
pianist born and raised in eastern North Carolina, wore a collard leaf in his
lapel as a sign of his African American identity. President Barack Obama
included collard greens on the menu at his first State Dinner.[16] There are
at least four collard festivals designed specifically to celebrate African
American heritage: Port Wentworth, Georgia, since 1997; East Palo Alto,
California, since 1998; Columbus, Ohio, first celebrated in August 2010;
and Atlanta, Georgia, starting in September 2011. The African American
organizers of the Columbus collard festival say it raises money for education,
health awareness, and other issues.[17] Collards can be a distinctive African
American cultural symbol for many people.

The novelist and poet Alice Walker, born and raised in Eatonton,
Georgia, used collards to speak about the modern experience of being an
African American woman: "America should have closed down on the first
day a black woman observed that supermarket collard greens tasted like
water."[18] Her comment may be about the quality of supermarket produce,
but it is also about collards. The flavor of homegrown collards is, for Walker,
strong enough to represent the cultural wealth of African American
heritage.

Collards are a key symbol in *Linden Hills* (1985), a critically acclaimed
novel by Gloria Naylor. In this work, the characters seek to join the upper
class in a Southern city. One crisis comes when the protagonist is selecting

the menu for a dinner party; collards and fried catfish are replaced with marinated shrimp and stuffed artichokes in an attempt to adopt the habits of the wealthy neighbors.[19] This rejection of collards is, for Naylor, a sign of the cultural malnourishment of some black Americans.

Even collards growing in a garden can be a powerful symbol for African Americans. The oppression of life under slavery may have been briefly relieved for some women and men in the time they were allowed away from their slave duties to cultivate a garden for their own family.[20] Some African American historians make the case that in these gardens (which must have included collard patches), men and women had creative opportunities to apply African gardening traditions.[21] They may also, it is assumed, have drawn spiritual and emotional strength from the gardening experience itself.[22]

Some African American scholars have attempted to explain why Walker, Monk, and others have chosen collards as positive symbols of their heritage. One such scholar of cooking suggested that collards serve as a reminder of past suffering: according to Rafia Zafar, "the eating of collards has meaning in ways analogous to the eating of parsley from a modern Seder plate: for Jewish and black people alike, the ingestion of bitter greens serves as a near-literal taste of slavery."[23] On the contrary, the people we interviewed often spoke of collard greens as comfort food, recalling happy memories of youth and satisfying times with family and community.

Historians tell us that West African cultures have long had a strong love of leafy greens and of vegetables in general. Jessica Harris, perhaps the leading historian of African American food, argues that leafy greens eaten in the American South have many important predecessors in West Africa.[24] Suffice it to say, then, that the collard serves as an effective symbol of sustenance.

African Americans in East Palo Alto, California, organized their first Collard Greens Festival in 1998. Founder Nobantu Ankoanda says that through many hard times, "it was a sustaining staple vegetable that kept us alive as a people." Collards have also been an important vegetable for millions of black Southerners and their descendants for over two centuries. Eating collards is a strong tradition in many African American celebrations.

Ella Woods of Evergreen, Alabama (see fig. 6) confides that she never imagined collards were just for black people. Like many, she thinks of collards as plainly Southern food. Organizers of several collard festivals—for example, those in Gaston, South Carolina, since 1982; Ponce de Leon, Florida, from 1980 to 1991; and the oldest and largest festival in Ayden, North Carolina, since 1975—don't consider the greens to be a racial symbol.

In Charlotte, North Carolina, the Latibah Collard Green Museum opened in 2010 near Highland Park on the north side. For five dollars, visitors may tour the community project, whose mission it is to educate local black Americans about their history. Quoting the website, Latibah is "a history museum comprised of a collection of installations, exhibits, and artifacts of fine art and cultural history. The museum covers key historical eras from the enslavement of Africans through the American systems of slavery, reconstruction, and integration to the (inauguration of the) 44th President of the U.S.A."[25] The name of the museum is symbolic, representing black culture in its entirety, not just food culture.

The national president of Sierra Club, Lisa Renstrom, has put collards to an innovative use: at a dinner party in her Charlotte home, guests were impressed with the buffet table centerpiece made of collards from Lisa's garden. Lisa said the greens wouldn't be wasted: they'd be part of the next day's dinner.[26]

Mistakes are made when anyone assumes collards are essentially a black food. At the end of the 1997 Masters Tournament in Augusta, Georgia, golfer Fuzzy Zoeller made a collard joke at the expense of winner Tiger Woods. At age 21, Woods was the youngest competitor to ever win, as well as the first African American to capture any major golf tournament. Referring to the tradition of allowing the tournament winner to select the menu for the players' banquet, Zoeller said to reporters, "That little boy is driving well and he's putting well. He's doing everything it takes to win. So, you know what you guys do when he gets in here? You pat him on the back and say congratulations and enjoy it and tell him not to serve fried chicken next year . . . or collard greens or whatever in the hell they serve." Zoeller at first defended his remark as a friendly jest but later apologized directly to Woods. Woods accepted the apology, but Zoeller's insensitive comments still cost him valuable sponsors.[27]

This incident points to how food is a culturally loaded domain in America. In January 2010, the Denver, Colorado, public school system had publicized a lunch menu intended to honor Dr. Martin Luther King Jr., featuring "Southern Style" chicken and collard greens. When some local African American residents complained that the action was racist, the school district removed the menu and apologized publically. The school district spokesman said the meal was "highly insensitive in light of certain hurtful cultural stereotypes still harbored in parts of our society."[28]

Or consider a controversy that made a brief news splash in February 2010. At NBC's employee cafeteria in New York City, chef Leslie Calhoun (who is African American) chose to celebrate Black History Month with a special lunch menu that included fried chicken, collard greens, and black-eyed peas, which Calhoun later said were foods she likes and considers proud elements of African American culture. But other African American employees complained, even going to the press with the claim that this decision was racist. Within 24 hours, NBC had replaced the special menu and apologized to their employees.[29]

The assumption among some white people that all black people like collards can indeed arise as a prejudice with hurtful intentions, as when people once insulted Irish people by referring to them "potato-eaters." The palatability of potatoes need not be impugned, and an Irish person might *well* be comforted by a dish made of potatoes, but it is thoughtless for any other person to *assume* that an Irish person *must* be so comforted, for this makes of that person a caricature. Patricia Turner's study of watermelons in American history is a detailed analysis (particularly through examinations of advertising art) of how one food has been used to stereotype African Americans. Turner shows how for over a century watermelons have been depicted and interpreted in ways that rationalize certain white prejudices: blacks are savages, oversexed, and well-fed.[30] Our research did not find examples of stereotypically racist collard advertising.

African American author David Lamb published a successful novel about relations between blacks and Latinos called *Do Platanos Go Wit' Collard Greens?* It became the basis of a successful Broadway play, *Platanos & Collard Greens.* Lamb is from New York City, where, unaware of the complexity of Southern foodways, it might be easy to assume that collards are *essentially* black folks' food just as platanos are *essentially* Latino food.

Dr. Martin Luther King Jr. made collards a quiet part of his story when he was in jail in Selma, Alabama. That building continues to stand as a landmark in the Civil Rights Movement, where protesters were put behind bars for organizing against the Jim Crow laws. Jailed there in February 1965, Dr. King published a letter from his cell, in which he said, "There are more negroes in jail with me than there are on the voting rolls." On his first night, a trustee of the jail offered him a plate of collards, but Dr. King turned them down. The trustee asked why, and Dr. King said that he and Dr. Ralph Abernathy had decided that, like Mohandas Gandhi, "We would make our prison sentences times of spiritual retreat. And to put ourselves into the proper frame of mind, we have always made it our practice that for the first two days that we are in jail, we will fast. That, my friend, is why I am unable to eat your greens."[31] We do not know whether Dr. King thought of collards as a symbol of black identity.

Collards may be said to have the fortitude to outlast misery in the memories of many Southerners. One of the most vivid descriptions of poverty in the South is by African American Richard Wright, who grew up in Jackson, Mississippi, during the 1910s and 1920s and endured neglect and cruelty at the hands of both white and black adults. His autobiography, *Black Boy: A Record of Childhood and Youth* (1945), brilliantly records his experience. One of his painful memories was of the weakness that came from being undernourished: "I knew . . . hunger that made my body aimlessly restless . . . hunger that made hate leap out of my heart like the dart of a serpent's tongue . . . No pork or veal was ever eaten . . . and rarely was there meat of any kind. We seldom ate fish and then only those that had scales and spines . . . For breakfast I ate mush and gravy made from flour and lard and for hours afterward I would belch it up into my mouth . . . At four o'clock in the afternoon I ate a plate of greens cooked with lard."[32] As a teenager he worked temporary jobs to bring the family larger food portions, but even then his meals were repetitive and limited: "The routine of the house flowed on as usual; for me there was sleep, mush, school, greens, study, loneliness, yearning, and then sleep again." He later reflected on how he survived, partly through the traditional wisdom he must have heard during his Mississippi youth: "Perhaps the sunshine, the fresh air, and the pot liquor from greens kept me going."

When he was old enough, Wright fled to the North and tried to make a home in Chicago and then New York City. Still, the South was in his soul: "I was not leaving the South to forget the South, but so that someday I might understand it." He did just that through his acclaimed works *Uncle Tom's Children* and *Native Son*. Even in northern cities, however, Wright met with bigotry and abuse. Finally, he found refuge in France, moving with his wife to an apartment in Paris and then to a quiet village in Normandy. In his last years, one particular food was never forgotten by this fugitive from the South. In a garden outside that French cottage, Wright grew collard greens.[33]

COLLARDS LINKED TO POVERTY AND/OR RURALITY

The poverty faced by the young Richard Wright may be related to the way collards have been derided elsewhere. Chuck Larkin, Georgia's most famous teller of traditional folktales, once told this joke about life during the Great Depression: "Poor has its limitations. One Thanksgiving, we had one baked sparrow stuffed with collard greens. That was the year we ate collard greens breakfast, lunch and dinner, week after week. We ate so many collard greens that when we went out to play, Momma tied kerosene rags around our ankles so the cut worms wouldn't eat us down."[34]

In 1898, Georgia Congressman J. M. Griggs made this statement before the House of Representatives: "I would not incite my friends . . . to riot, but I must say that a dinner of hog jowls and sweet Georgia collards, or bacon and tender spring turnip tops, or fried chicken and brown gravy, with the inseparable accompaniment of sugar yams, smoking corn pones, hot biscuits, and cold buttermilk, is better than all the pork and beans or corned beef and pickled cabbage, pumpkin pies, stale bread, and cider that can be spread on any table in New England."[35] The congressman's defensive tone may reflect the general southern bitterness toward the more powerful North, but more likely Griggs is presuming a northern disdain for southern rurality, for which collards make a tidy example. Why? There are many vegetables that could have become such a symbol. Cabbage, in fact, has been mocked as a food of the poor and, particularly, of the Irish poor. Mark Twain claimed that cauliflower was "nothing but cabbage with a college education," which seems to assign cabbage a lower status, at least ironically.[36] Americans honor spinach's symbolic role as the fuel for great Popeye-like strength. Sweet corn, lettuce, carrots, and tomatoes have mostly positive images. Even if they might periodically be made into comic props—corn for provinciality, tomatoes as weapons of the riffraff—they are internationally popular for sweetness, bright color, and versatility in cooking. Although okra and grits are also occasionally derided as foods of insult, informal evidence suggests that collards play the larger role.

FLANNERY O'CONNOR: COLLARDS AND CLASS

A single collard leaf is central to Flannery O'Connor's short story "A Stroke of Good Fortune," first published in 1949. The main character in this story is an unhappy and self-absorbed working-class woman. Her unhappiness is in large part due to her unfulfilled dreams of joining the middle class. She is deeply embarrassed that her brother has retained his rustic habits in spite of having traveled the world as a sailor during the war. As the story opens, she has just returned from the grocery store, where she reluctantly bought collard greens at his request. As she enters her apartment, she sees her reflection in the window. Bringing the reflected image into focus, she discovers that she has a piece of collard leaf stuck to her cheek. Horrified, she swipes at it and curses her brother.[37]

The collard leaf seems to represent the trap of her working-class position. She sees collards as a food of shame due to their association in the minds of many with the condition of poverty. O'Connor's use of the collard leaf as a symbol suggests that by the late 1940s this association was recognizable, at least at a regional scale and perhaps at a national one. There is nothing in the story to suggest the characters' race, and the story makes no reference to black culture. So the association here should be seen solely as one between poverty and collard greens. Perhaps O'Connor's Savannah in the 1940s was a cultural region where all citizens (but mostly poor ones) enjoyed eating collards.

Perhaps the cheapness of collards, like cabbage, lends them their lower-class association. The greater expense of pecans, artichoke hearts, and other uncommon foods could give them some caché among the elite, at least in the past. Particular vegetables are seldom linked to social class, race, or regional identity—but, for some reason, collards are. Beginning in the nineteenth century, there are many references to collard greens that imply a link to poverty or, at least, to less "refined" ways of life. It is only gradually that some begin to defend collards from disparagement and even to celebrate them.

Rural folk generally ignore the insults sent in their direction by jokes and barbs. Many know that the value of collards sometimes extends beyond eating them. Witness this folk-medicine use reputed to have taken place in a Nashville hospital in 1972:

My baby boy was sick and in the hospital, and he was sharing his
room with another baby, a black boy no more than four weeks old,
who had a high fever. Nothing could bring down that boy's fever. I
thought he would die, such a frail baby. One night, I was lying in the

chair by my son's bed, and I heard the boy's family come in and I saw them close the curtain around the baby's bed. I couldn't tell what they were doing in there. After a while there was an awful smell, like nothing I had ever known. I finally got the courage to peek: they had wrapped that boy entirely in collard leaves, and his fever was heating up those leaves, almost cooking them. They stood around that boy and watched him and prayed over him. I don't know how much time passed, and I suppose I slept again, but I know when morning came that boy's fever was gone and he was okay. We were very happy for that family. I'll never forget that day . . . or that smell.[38]

In eastern North Carolina, several elderly informants recounted a widespread practice called "collard stealing," a Christmas season recreational activity that author Morgan's aunt Doris indicated lasted at least until the 1940s and 1950s. Groups of teenagers would spend hours on a cold December night walking the dirt roads and trails of their rural communities to play tricks on people thought to be either wealthy or eccentric. In a few areas the folk game was "practiced" in early January as a part of the celebration of Old Christmas. According to Aunt Doris, here is how the trick was accomplished: A few mature collard plants would be pulled from a roadside garden and then taken to a nearby residence and dropped on the front steps. The celebrating youths would then knock on the door of the unsuspecting recipients of the collards, yell loudly, and run away. The offended residents would answer the door to discover their gift of collards. During the hard times of the Great Depression, the practice of collard stealing was sometimes feigned by teens bringing stolen collards to their own homes and leaving them on their steps or porches. Their unsuspecting parents would discover the collards the next morning and think they were left by mischievous neighbor kids. Then, of course, they would cook and eat the collards.

Wherever and however the collard is celebrated—whether in poetry, festival, song, literature, or even folk medicine—it is usually in a simple but treasured down-home way. Yes, some people hate the smell of cooking collards, while others consider the green to be pure comfort food. No matter; eating collards is anticipated with intense salivation by millions of the vegetable's admirers.

2

Eating Collards

The Reasons We Do or Don't

A college student in South Carolina told us this story:
*I remember the first time my girlfriend served me collard greens—and I
was afraid of them, really. I thought she was feeding me seaweed! But I
had to try them, out of respect. The strong flavor was a bit of a shock, but
I came to love the greens after the second time, and now I even crave them
sometimes. My parents back in Pennsylvania don't understand.*

How to put into words the experience of eating collards! The flavor is
stronger than that of cooked cabbage, almost meaty by comparison. It's not
the same as spinach, for the texture of collards is more "al dente," or perhaps
"involving." No, collards are not delicate, and that's part of their appeal. The
flavor seems to linger, like that of a good ale. The characteristic texture is
essential to the experience: collard lovers seem to find a deep pleasure in
how they "play." A parallel experience could be found in bass fishing. If the
hooked fish just rolls over and gives up the fight, there is hardly a memory
of catching it; but if that fish tries mightily to swim away, making a game
of it, the fisherman is pleased to join in the chase and has a story to tell

back home. Likewise, good collards engage the diner. When they are not so overcooked that they melt in the mouth, they provide appreciators with a positive masticating experience unlike any other food.

In this chapter we contrast collards with other greens and offer stories about eating collards, some going back to the Civil War. We also explain about the importance of collards to nutrition, beginning with more unscientific ideas about what collards can do for—and to—a person. Southerners know that eating greens introduces to a digestive system something more than fiber, calcium, and a slightly bitter flavor—it also engages forces one cannot always comprehend.

In 1890, Arkansas writer Opie Read related a story about a white preacher in Jefferson County who had argued uncharacteristically with a church member. The incident left both men with feelings of self-reproach. Some days later the preacher met his friend on the street and apologized, saying, "It wasn't my mind that was talking . . . it was an overindulgence in collard greens." The friend was greatly relieved and said that it had been the same with him. "Thank God," said he. "It was just collard greens talking!"[1]

Collards are painted as even more dangerous in a very old Louisiana story recorded by Dr. Henry C. Lewis. This doctor, who lived from 1825 to 1850, was a keen observer of early Louisiana. Attempting to reproduce dialect, Lewis has a black man tell the tale of a sick neighbor who had "takin awfil sick arter etin a bate of cold fride collards." A doctor arrived and had the family create an infusion of "pepper pods and lobely." As this was being prepared, however, a screech owl hollered. "I sed then as I say now . . . that it war a sine and a forerunner that she was gwine to die." The doctor gave the woman the tea to drink anyway. "Well, the first dose that he gin her didn't 'fect much, so he gin her another pint, an' then cummenst stemin' her, when the pirspirashun began to kum out, she sunk rite down, an' begun to siken awful; the cold fride collards began to kum up in gobs, but Blessed Master! it war too late, the screech owl had hollered, an' she flung up cold fride collards till she dide, pooer creetur! The Lord be marsyful to her poor soul!"[2] This story suggests that collards were widely known in the

Deep South by the 1840s. One hopes we have long since grown out of any fear that eating a cold dish of collards might kill us. We now live in a world where greens in general are highly respected for their nutritional aspects.

COLLARDS IN THE PARADE OF GREENS

Collards compete for attention with several other cooked greens. Americans also eat spinach, turnip greens, mustard greens, and kale, and some even eat dandelion greens, creasy greens, rutabaga greens, and pokeberry greens. New greens, such as arugula and mesclun, were introduced in recent decades by immigrants and adventurous souls. Spinach holds the top national ranking.

In the South, however, only turnips come close to collards in popularity. Turnips have a particular advantage over nearly every other garden crop in that there are two foods in one plant: the leaves can be harvested for greens first, and then the turnip root later. Many gardeners harvest them at the same time and cook and eat the leaves and root together. Partly for these reasons, turnips have often been seen as an essential food among country folk in the North and South since before the Civil War.[3] Perhaps because they are so easily stored and transported, there are records of root turnips having been a standard source of nutrition consumed throughout the South by both armies and civilians. The greens themselves are, however, less commonly mentioned in those reports.[4]

Authentic turnip greens, many believe, should include diced turnip roots. They say the turnips give the greens better flavor and texture—but maybe it's the other way around. There are some turnip festivals in the United States, mostly in New England. The only turnip *greens* festival we found is in the tiny town of Easton, Texas. And, yes, they cook their turnip greens with diced turnips.

To place collards in the context of all the other leading greens, see table 1.

Spinach is by far the most popular green in the United States, rising through the ranks of all vegetables (Alma, Arkansas, actually has a spinach festival now). Among other leafy greens, collards came in a distant second, closely followed by turnip, mustard, and kale. This ranking is confirmed by a nonscientific poll of food professionals by the Culinary Institute of America in 2011, which asked "What are your favorite kinds of greens?" Spinach was number one at 32 percent, collards came in second at 15 percent, followed by chard, kale, mesclun, and other.[5] Of course, chard and mesclun are relatively new to the scene, and it is hard to guess whether they are simply flashes in the pan. Collards have been popular greens for centuries.

Notice that since the 1990s, except for spinach, the per capita consumption of greens seems to have declined (mesclun and chard volumes are lowest). But are these greens really in decline? Like collards, this data should be taken with more than a grain of salt. The increase in sales of prechopped greens as opposed to bunches of whole leaves with stems may mask stable consumption levels or even an actual increase in consumption.

TABLE 1. CONSUMPTION OF THE MAIN LEAFY GREENS AS
REPORTED BY THE US DEPARTMENT OF AGRICULTURE*

Type	1998	1999	2000	2001	2002
Spinach	1.9	1.8	2.0	2.2	1.8
Collard	0.8	0.8	0.8	0.8	0.8
Turnip	0.5	0.5	0.5	0.4	0.5
Mustard	0.7	0.7	0.7	0.8	0.7
Kale	0.4	0.4	0.4	0.4	0.3

With the new and very popular prechopped greens sold in bags, a consumer can buy smaller quantities of greens and still get as much to eat as when they bought whole bunches; the uneaten portion of a whole bunch (such as stems) may average 40 percent. Also, note that eating collards grown at home is not counted in these estimates of consumption. Even greens bought from a local grower are likely to be missed. In addition, the time period of this data (1998 to 2008) is too short to allow any prediction.

People's dietary habits may be worse now than in the past, as evidenced by the rise in obesity, but we must beware of romanticizing the past, or lumping all classes together. It appears that those who could afford to eat luxuries, such as sweets or plentiful beef, would eat them at the expense of their vegetables. Collards and other greens are mentioned only rarely in the dietaries of wealthy families. During the nineteenth century, however, a poor southern family was said to eat with the seasons, while the upper class treated such an approach as primitive.

2003	2004	2005	2006	2007	2008
2.3	2.6	2.6	2.8	2.8	2.5
0.9	0.8	0.7	0.6	0.5	0.4
0.5	0.5	0.4	0.4	0.4	0.3
0.8	0.8	0.7	0.6	0.4	0.3
0.4	0.4	0.3	0.3	0.3	0.3

*Recorded as pounds per person, per year. These estimates are based only on what is sold at the retail level. The USDA Economic Research Service recognizes that after food has been purchased at a store or restaurant, some portion is uneaten.

The upper class may have been particularly loath to eat not just collards but indeed any vegetables. Sarah Morgan, a wealthy woman forced by the Civil War to live away from her Louisiana home and to suffer various inconveniences, wrote in her diary in 1863: "Absurd as it may seem, I think my first act on my return home, will be to take a cup of coffee, and a piece of bread, two luxuries of which I have been deprived for a long while. How many articles we considered as absolutely necessary, before, have we now been obliged to dispense with! . . . Ice cream, lemonade and sponge cake was my chief diet; it was a year last July since I tasted the two first, and one since I have seen the latter. Bread I believed necessary to life; vegetables, useless. The former I never see and I have been forced into cultivating at least a toleration of the latter. Snap beans I can actually swallow, sweet potatoes I really like, and one day at Dr. Nolan's I 'bolted' a mouthful of tomatoes and afterwards kept my seat with the heroism of a martyr."[6]

Vegetables can be mocked more easily, perhaps, when a writer is looking for something an audience will find strange. An example is found in a travelogue from 1934, *Stars Fell on Alabama*, a national best seller for Carl Carmer, who had moved from New York City to Tuscaloosa to teach at the University of Alabama. He stayed for seven years and then wrote about his travels around the state, speaking warmly of many Alabama traditions. But he complains in the book about three foods in particular that he says were both ubiquitous and unpleasant: okra, cornbread, and collard greens.[7]

The Civil War and Collards

In considering more deeply the roots of our current collard habit, it is necessary to turn to the most powerful collective memories of Southerners—those associated with the Civil War. In an article in the journal *Southern Exposure*, a cultural historian made the case that "perhaps more than any foods save cornbread and barbecue, collard greens have come to symbolize the distinctive tastes of the South . . . One reason was that they had fed the region through slavery and civil war."[8]

Although no primary documents to support this last audacious claim have been found, certainly food shortages in the South were well known, and troops from both sides regularly "requisitioned" garden produce as they marched past farmsteads. Winter gardens, many of which would have contained collards, turnips, cabbage, or mustard greens, were an easy and very noticeable target for hungry soldiers, who would have hardly resisted taking these greens if they had access to some boiling water for cooking. The mother of one of the authors, Lucy Claytor Davis, grew up during the 1930s and 1940s in Waycross and Augusta, Georgia, and recalled hearing her elders say that during the war collards were especially helpful to have in a kitchen garden because "that was a crop no Yankee soldier would eat."

There are, however, many documented cases of Confederate soldiers appreciating collards; there are twenty-six primary documents that mention soldiers eating collards during the war. Here are a few stories, mostly from Georgia:

A minor scandal occurring during General William T. Sherman's "March to the Sea" involved Georgia Governor Joseph Brown. He was rumored to have fled the temporary state capitol in Milledgeville ignominiously, bringing his cow and a load of collards while abandoning important state property to the Yankees. A Confederate officer who had served under Brown wrote years later in his defense, "I discovered a luxuriant lot of collards in the garden; and without the knowledge of Governor Brown or his wife I ordered Aunt Celia, an old colored cook, to cut and bring them to where the wagons were being loaded . . . knowing the Governor's family would need part of them while refugeeing from place to place."[9]

In August 1862, the *Savannah Republican* newspaper ran a request that residents donate food to local hospitals: "Vegetables of every kind . . . and collards even will be most gratefully received. Convalescent men have to be fed and strengthened, and their appetites crave their old familiar home diet . . . New sweet potatoes will be coming on—you could not send them a greater luxury."[10]

In April 1864, a soldier camped near Atlanta reported that he received a meal of "Irish potatoes, Blue collards, and tomatoes, besides our ration of beef and cornbread."[11]

A. J. Matthews of Atlanta heard from her grandmother that her ancestor Isaac Blackshear was captured by the enemy and sent to prison in New York, where he was fed nothing but a thin soup, and, after the war, "made his way back to his home in Twiggs County, a walking skeleton . . . .When he came home, the women folks were preparing dinner and had a huge pot of collard greens cooking and . . . he couldn't wait until they were done, but ate the whole pot-full half cooked."

The prison hospital at Andersonville (Sumter County, Georgia), where many Union soldiers died, was able to offer its prisoners only a poor diet, mostly "boiled beef, rice, molasses, and coarse corn bread baked without sifting . . . To this we sometimes . . . added a small allowance of vegetables, such as peas, potatoes, and collards. These [were] generally issued raw and the patients . . . compelled to hire their comrades to cook them in some sort of style and pay them out of their scanty allowance."[12]

Food shortages were sometimes critical, as reported in a prominent Confederacy newspaper, the *Daily Southern Crisis* (Jackson, Mississippi) in February 1863. The editors wrote that "the army has suffered more from lack of vegetables than of clothing, shoes or medicine . . . We have never seen any portion of the habitable globe so afflicted for the want of vegetable supplies as the States of the Southwest." The journal editors suggested that "the usual meat ration of 3½ lbs per week for slaves could be sharply reduced by substituting squash, collards and tomatoes and by increasing the proportion of sorghum molasses."[13] Note that it is the slaves' diet, not the soldiers', that is to be cut.

The "Hill Country" of north central Louisiana is centered in five parishes: Claiborne, Lincoln, Union, Jackson, and Bienville. In this sector, the people consider themselves different from the rest of Louisiana. Few French influences are felt, the connection to British and Protestant traditions is somewhat self-conscious, and small farms still dot the land. Quite a few collard patches persist. Thomas Sylvest, raised in Natchitoches Parish (just south of the Hill Country) in the 1930s, self-published a book titled *Collard Greens*, naming it for the green vegetable he had eaten the most.[14] Collards seem to have been a standard dish in Louisiana's Hill Country since the nineteenth century, although visitors from elsewhere were not impressed. In 1869, geographer Samuel Lockett wrote disparagingly about the food he found there: "Three times a day for nearly 365 days a year, their simple meal is coarse corn bread and fried bacon. At dinner there will be added perhaps collards or some other coarse vegetable. Even when they have fresh meat of venison, which they can obtain whenever they wish, it is always fried and comes to the table swimming in a sea of clear, melted lard."[15] Although he was a Southerner, born in Virginia and raised in Alabama, Lockett seems to have considered collards beneath him.

Local folk seem to have been more positive in their attitude toward collards and fried bacon. During the Civil War, Henry T. Morgan, a private from Claiborne Parish, wrote to his wife in October 1862: "Ellen wee have a hard time hear. Beef and bread is our diet. I dont no what i wood give fore a mess of bacon and collards."[16]

Another sign of a long-standing collard tradition is the Louisiana Sweet collard, a kind of collard that old seed savers around the South often mention. A 1934 publication called "Collards: A Truck Crop for Louisiana," published by the Agricultural Experiment Station at Louisiana State University, describes the Louisiana Sweet as something the station's breeders were hoping to make into a stable form of collard. Their reasoning was that commercial growers need a collard plant that is consistent, which they argued would make a "more attractive product for the grocer's shelves."[17] The breeding program appears to have been discontinued: in our travels and research, the Louisiana Sweet collard remained as elusive as a ghost. Photos from the 1934 publication show the plant to have short stems and a more compact center. Some plant experts suggested that a gardener might call their collard by that name even if it were a common variety; plant naming is notoriously imprecise. Still, the Louisiana Sweet collard may be out there somewhere, preserved by seed savers, perhaps kept as a precious secret.

In the town of Ruston, Louisiana, a wonderful cook and writer named Mary Cheatham has made collards into a major success story. She co-wrote with Paul Elliott a book of collard recipes and stories called *The Collard Patch* (2006).[18] The book has sold well on Amazon.com and she continues to share her passion for collards and other healthful foods. Cheatham says, "We all know that the body is the temple of the soul . . . and collard greens are one of the most nutritious vegetables available. What better way is there to take care of our bodies—and honor God—than to dig into a plate of collards?" Cheatham's recipe for collards, titled "Red River Gumbo," is featured in Chapter Three.

One famous Mississippi collard lover must be mentioned here: Elvis Presley, born and raised in Tupelo. Although Elvis became world famous, traveling widely, he retained his Southern food preferences. Mary Jenkins, who cooked for him for many years, told a *Newsweek* reporter that she fed him meals fit for a hardworking farmer—or maybe three farmers. She said, "If he wanted collard greens, I'd have to make a whole skillet of cornbread, and take it up to him with a half-gallon of buttermilk."[19]

In fact, collards have also been blamed for some unhealthy eating habits among less famous people. For example, Roosevelt Wilson, the principal of Selma (Alabama) High School, made a surprising announcement to a *Christian Science Monitor* journalist in 2006: "If I could, I'd tell our people never to eat collards again."[20] His reason? Collard greens are cooked with too much fat and represent a wider set of unhealthy food traditions in his community. Although the article does honor southern and black foodways, the reporter, with the principal, denounced the following southern foods: collards, fried chicken, pulled pork, crawfish pies, bacon-soaked beans, corn pone, red link sausages, chicken fried steak, red-eye gravy, brains with eggs, fried chitterlings, molasses, fried catfish, barbecue, smoked sausage, and grits with lots of butter. Why, out of all these dishes, are collards the one vegetable labeled as an unhealthy food?

Many people assume that collards are always cooked with pork fat—and lots of it—and many recipes and historical references to traditional cooking support this assumption. Doctors have been complaining about the high fat in southern cooking since at least 1860.[21] For poor, hardworking farm families, collards cooked with a bit of pork may have been one of the best possible sources of nutrition, providing protein, calcium, and antioxidants. Even the pot liquor, poured on cornbread, had—and still has—excellent nutritional value.[22]

A good gardener often offers valuable cooking hints. For example, Sarah Harper, who grows collards in Gainesville, Alabama, with her husband, 73-year-old Lemon "Lightning" Harper, includes chopped green pepper when she cooks the collards, and, according to "Lightning," "it makes all the difference." He brags that his wife really "knows what she's doing." Harper said he eats collards at least every week when they are in season and other greens the rest of the year. He said that greens are what a body needs. Such ideas are not based on reading health magazines, where articles like "The Hottest New Vegetable Sources of Vitamins and Minerals" are found, but rather on the wisdom of sage elders, passed down to younger generations.

Judy Sellers, in her 30s, has lived in the tiny town of Orrville, Alabama, all her life. She works in the town's only country store—which sells mostly beer, junk foods, and lottery tickets—but she doesn't eat anything from the store. Sellers said she grew up with "better food than that. I make greens all the time—collard, turnip, mustard—and sometimes cabbage. We don't grow a garden like my grandma did, but I know how to cook better than most everybody—that's what my husband tells me anyway! He'll tell you collards are the best thing I make." She admitted that she cooks hers with pork fat. But Sellers has "cut way down on the amount of fat in that pot." Times change; the myth of Southerners eating only the fattiest versions of collards is not a fair judgment.

NUTRITION AND COLLARDS

So, how healthy is a dish of collards? The science of nutrition is a developing one, and much is still unknown about exactly how different nutrients function to keep us healthy. But the US Department of Agriculture's Nutrition Database shows that collards compare favorably with the four other major leafy greens and cabbage (see table 2).

Collards rank higher than the other leafy greens or cabbage in seven nutrients: fiber, calcium, niacin, vitamin B5, choline, carotene-alpha, and cryptoxanthin-beta. Collards rank second in protein, iron, magnesium, phosphorus, zinc, manganese, riboflavin, folate, and vitamin K. Certain nutrients might be found in higher amounts in the other greens, and, overall, it seems spinach may have the nutritional edge, but collards are superior to cabbage, turnip greens, mustard greens, and kale.

Freda Butner, a registered dietitian and marketing specialist for the North Carolina Department of Agriculture and Consumer Services, says many people have misperceptions about collards, the number one being that collards are always cooked with pork fat. She promotes the use of lower-fat meats as flavoring or even suggests completely meatless collard recipes. "Some people buy packages of turkey wings, thinking they are healthier, but those are often just as high in fat as pork is," she said.

Butner also worries that reports of a connection to kidney stones have scared people away from collards. "Caucasian southern men have a particularly high incidence of kidney stones, and, taking a blood thinner (properly called anticoagulant) for their heart, are often told not to eat leafy greens. The substances at fault here are oxalates," she said, "which lead to calcium precipitates in a body's system—the main cause of kidney stones. Oxalates are found not only in all the dark leafy greens, but also in strawberries, and even sweet tea and soda." Doctors should point out to patients that, of all the leafy greens, collards have a far lower oxalate concentration. "Consider that a half cup of cooked collards has 74 milligrams of oxalates. A half cup of kale will contain 125 milligrams, and chard has 660 milligrams. And the same amount of spinach has 750 milligrams!" So not all leafy greens are the same. Will eating a cup of collards every day increase the risk of kidney stones? "Not if they are cooked right. What increases a patient's risk is being overweight, eating too much salt, eating too much animal protein, not drinking enough water, or excessive heat exposure. Doesn't that sound like some men you know? And maybe if a doctor mentions cutting back on certain foods, and the list includes both leafy greens and red meat, the patient will choose to cut out the leafy greens."

Butner also noted that the benefits from eating collards are astonishing. "One essential nutrient you don't hear enough about is folate. Deficiency in this ingredient can lead to anemia, depression, slow growth rates in children, and premature births. "So eat collards, friends," she said, "because a cup of collards is an excellent source of folate."

The value of collards has been recognized in a number of medical studies. Findings from the medical field for the nutrients in which collards rank very high include:

- Fiber: lowers risk of coronary heart disease[23]
- Calcium: lowers risk of obesity[24]
- Niacin: lowers risk of coronary disease mortality[25]
- Pantothenic acid: may improve the healing of wounds[26]
- Carotene-alpha: lowers risk of premature death[27]
- Cryptoxanthin: increases survival from some cancers[28]

These studies are being used to promote greens in the broad effort to confront obesity, diabetes, osteoporosis, and other diseases. Yet there seems to be a need to reeducate some who have known collards. For example, the rise in calcium deficiency has led nutritionist Dr. Yvonne Bronner to call for a "return to traditional greens." She says she can recall when most African Americans that she knew ate collard or mustard greens at least two or three times a week, thereby getting the calcium they needed, even if they avoided milk because of lactose intolerance.[29] A national dietary study conducted

TABLE 2. COLLARD GREENS' NUTRITION COMPARED WITH OTHER LEAFY GREENS

Nutrient	Units	1 Cup Cooked Collard	% of Recommended Daily Intake
Protein	g	4.01	8%
Fiber	g	5.3	21%
Calcium	mg	266	27%
Iron	mg	2.2	12%
Magnesium	mg	38	10%
Phosphorus	mg	57	6%
Potassium	mg	220	5%
Zinc	mg	0.44	3%
Copper	mg	0.072	4%
Manganese	mg	0.828	41%
Selenium	mcg	0.9	1%
Vitamin C	mg	34.6	58%
Thiamin	mg	0.076	5%
Riboflavin	mg	0.201	12%
Niacin	mg	1.092	5%
Vitamin B5	mg	0.414	4%
Vitamin B6	mg	0.243	12%
Folate	mcg	177	44%
Choline	mg	60.4	14%
Carotene, beta	mcg	9147	*
Carotene, alpha	mcg	171	*
Cryptoxanthin, beta	mcg	38	*
Viatmin A	IU	15417	100%
Lutein & Zeaxanthin	mcg	14619	*
Vitamin E	mg	1.67	11%
Vitamin K	mcg	836	100%

*The FDA has not set a daily recommended intake level for these nutrients.

1 Cup Cooked Turnip	1 Cup Cooked Mustard	1 Cup Cooked Kale	1 Cup Cooked Cabbage	1 Cup Cooked Spinach
1.64	3.16	2.47	1.9	5.35
5	2.8	2.6	2.8	4.3
197	104	94	72	245
1.15	0.98	1.17	0.26	6.43
32	21	23	22	157
42	57	36	50	101
292	283	296	294	839
0.2	0.15	0.31	0.3	1.37
0.364	0.118	0.203	0.026	0.313
0.485	0.384	0.541	0.308	1.683
1.3	0.8	1.2	1	2.7
39.5	35.4	53.3	56.2	17.6
0.065	0.057	0.069	0.092	0.171
0.104	0.088	0.091	0.058	0.425
0.592	0.606	0.65	0.372	0.882
0.395	0.168	0.064	0.26	0.261
0.259	0.137	0.179	0.168	0.436
170	102	17	44	263
0	0.4	0.5	30.4	35.5
6588	5312	10625	72	11318
0	0	0	0	0
0	0	0	0	0
10980	8852	17707	120	18866
12154	8347	23720	40	20354
2.71	1.69	1.1	0.22	3.74
529.3	419.3	0	163	888.5

Sources: USDA Nutrition Database, http://www.nal.usda.gov/fnic/foodcomp/search/ and Linus Pauling Institute, http://lpi.oregonstate.edu/infocenter/phytochemicals/carotenoids/index.html#sources

from 1988 to 1994 found that the rural white population had a lower intake of greens than those in urban areas.[30] So even as nutritionists are identifying the benefits of a diet rich in leafy greens, there seems to be a decline in the traditional greens culture among all Americans. A southern tradition may be on the way out, and with it the very basis of our good health.

3

Cooking Collards

Kitchen Stories and Home Recipes

The basic collard recipe requires just a few words: *Boil a ham hock in a large pot of water. Wash, tear, and add the leaves. Simmer till tender.* But good cooking is never as simple as that. Prior to 1970, few cookbooks offered a collard recipe, but it's certain that folks were cooking and eating collards before then. Good cooks were surely following diverse methods that maximized the positive flavors of the greens. So why weren't cookbook authors bothering to share their methods in print? Not because collards were too easy to cook. Simply boiling two or three ingredients may seem elemental, but gourmands know that collards are easily botched by poor cooking. So how do cooks successfully prepare collards?

The most important step is finding good collard leaves. The leaves begin to wilt once harvested and wilt rapidly in temperatures above approximately 50 degrees Fahrenheit or if exposed to dry air. This helps explain why many people keep a large garden where they can pick the leaves just before cooking them and why collards are traditionally a fall and winter crop.

The second most important consideration in cooking tasty collards is adding flavoring to the greens—traditionally pork, but lately a great variety of meats and spices. Collards won't taste good if they're simply boiled in water.

The final element is caution in the cooking time. Cook collards too little, and they'll be hard to chew; cook them too long, and they'll be brownish, slimy, and odd-tasting. Annie Morgan, the mother of this book's coauthor, John T. Morgan, prepares hers in the manner illustrated in figures 4a through 4d.

Collards are generally eaten with other food partners in traditional southern fare. For example, collards and cornbread make a very popular pairing, dating back to at least the early 1800s. And collards are also commonly paired with fried chicken or pork chops, even as modern foodways have made the frying pan less standard of late.

Collard Cooks

In Evergreen, Alabama, three generous souls identified the best local cook as Ella Woods, famous for her collards. Her friend Luther Upton, a local radio celebrity, took us to visit her on the covered porch of her small brick home, backed by a large, well-kept garden. We had already seen some grand purplish collards growing as ornamentals in a brick planter in her front yard (see fig. 6).

Over 80 years old, Woods is still a strong woman. She won't eat restaurant food ("can't trust it")—and prefers to avoid the grocery store. She often works alone in the garden and in handling her chickens and hog. Her philosophy: "Good food is food you grow for yourself and cook for yourself . . . and for your neighbors. If people would take the time to do that, you and I know we would be a whole lot healthier." When we asked her about how to cook collards, she said, "First, you go raise a hog, then come back and see me." When asked if she might kindly skip that part, she spelled out her detailed recipe for collards, which appears later in this chapter.

For some people, collards are simply a delivery system for strong spices. In the Southwest Arkansas town of Benton, we found Michael Roberts, a good cook raised in the Mississippi River delta whose people still live around the Crossett area. Through much trial and error, Roberts has created a slow-cooked collard dish that appears later in this chapter, filed under "Arkansas" and titled "Spicy Collards."

In the early twentieth century, a number of Chinese families settled in the delta in northwestern Mississippi. In fact, the 1950 census showed more Chinese people in this area than in any other part of the South. Most of these families, like many other folks who once lived there, have migrated to cities like Memphis or Jackson. But the remnants of their cultural contributions persist—with the last name of Chow still common in a few counties—as do some interesting recipes for greens. The most famous is one that was chosen for the Smithsonian Folklife Festival in 1997 in Washington, DC, where Gilroy Chow and his family were awarded the chance to cook their version of collards, stir-fried with oyster sauce. This recipe was also included in a 2003 *New York Times* article about the Chow family written by food historian Joan Nathan.[1]

Ann Weeks of Dunn, North Carolina, has determined the best way to freeze collards: First, prepare the collards fresh as though they would be consumed immediately. Then "dry them out"—that is, put them in a colander and press a small plate down on them. Place servings in quart-sized sealable plastic bags. This method seals in the flavor, so when thawed, the collards just need to be warmed up (you may have to add a little grease to the frying pan). Ann and her husband, David, run a small commercial collard farm, so they eat collards two or three times a week in winter and at least once a week out of season.

Collard Cooking History

Collard recipes seem to have been left out of the few cookbooks published in the eighteenth and nineteenth centuries. One such cookbook, the earliest known (1881) by an African American woman, is Abby Fisher's *What Mrs. Fisher Knows about Old Southern Cooking*[2] and does not include a recipe for greens. Another early cookbook, the *Virginia Cookery-Book* (1885 and later editions) by Mary Stuart Smith, again does not mention collards. Further, her mention of cabbage is not favorable: "This vegetable, so staple an article of food among out-of-door workers, has fallen into general disuse with the upper classes on account of the disagreeable odor it emits, permeating every corner of an ordinarily constructed house from garret to cellar."[3] What she thought of cooking collards one can only imagine.

African American cooks, who seldom had access to publishing houses, convey little data on the recipes they used before the mid-twentieth century.[4] During the decades of slavery, these cooks kept no diaries (or their diaries were lost), so there is even less documentation of cooking practices then. Cookbooks are being collected at a fast clip now, however, and hopefully someone will discover a cookbook from the nineteenth century that includes a collard recipe.[5]

One of the best-known records of African American cooking is Freda De Knight's *A Date with a Dish: A Cook Book of American Negro Recipes* (1948).[6] De Knight was the food editor for *Ebony* magazine just after World War II and sought to liberate black women from what she saw as the constraints of traditional foodways of the rural South. Her recipes are almost defensively non-Southern and often reflect white middle-class preferences. Whatever her motives, she includes no recipe for greens of any kind. The determination to escape Southern oppression and all its associations was a strong motivation to leave collards (and their history) behind. Fortunately, by the 1960s, African Americans were publicly embracing their southern roots and foodways.

In the 1960s and 1970s, soul food was not just a cuisine but also a movement to build self-respect among African Americans. Bob Jeffries, a successful chef living in Harlem, published one of the first soul food cookbooks in 1969. Jeffries had been raised in Alabama and had moved to New York City in search of fame as a singer and dancer, only to find that he could make more money with his cooking skills. In the preface of his cookbook, he wrote, "When people ask me about soul food, I tell them that

I have been cooking 'soul' for over forty years—only we did not call it that back home. We just called it real good cooking, southern style. However, if you want to be real technical on the subject, while all soul food is southern food, not all southern food is 'soul.'" Jeffries goes on to explain that soul food is no-frills, lacking in ornament but made with sincerity. The soul cook knows how to use herbs and spices, and yet keeps things simple and honest, cooking "chickens from their own back yard and collard greens they grew themselves." He includes a recipe for greens, explaining that you might use "collard greens, mustard greens, beet tops, kale, cabbage and carrot tops (any or all)."[7]

COLLARD RECIPES FROM AROUND THE SOUTH

Recipes are a unique form of writing, not like other nonfiction but more like a quick peek into someone else's kitchen, where one of our most powerful human experiences—the making and eating of food—is brought to light. For the longtime cook, there is much that is left unsaid, and skills are hidden between the lines. So it is with collards: when someone says "add a pinch of baking soda" the unstated understanding is that doing this will help any green vegetables keep their brighter color as they are being boiled.

Included are recipes from most Southern states (the states are listed here in alphabetical order).

ALABAMA

Collards by Ella Woods of Evergreen

"You can go buy a hog jowl if you have to. People don't believe me, but garlic is easy to grow here, and everybody knows that hot green peppers are easy to grow as well. I recommend using baking soda when cooking these collards, especially in the summer as it makes the leaves taste better."

1 small hog jowl, salted for about 2 weeks
1 bunch of collard leaves, about one pound
1 clove garlic, mashed
1 small hot green pepper, chopped
1 tablespoon sugar
1 tablespoon meat tenderizer
1 teaspoon baking soda

Boil the meat for 30 minutes in a large pot half-filled with water. Meanwhile carefully wash the leaves to remove any sand. Cut the collards into fine pieces—this is important for the texture. Put them in the pot with the meat and cook on high for 30 minutes. Then lower the heat to medium and stir. Add the garlic, hot pepper, sugar, meat tenderizer, and baking soda.

Cook as long as it takes for the collards to get tender, which depends entirely on the collards and the time of year. Summer collards take longer because they are tougher. Big leaves take longer than small young ones. Don't cook them too long, or you'll take all the goodness out. Stir every now and then. Reserve the pot liquor for cooking cornbread.

ALABAMA

Spicy Collards in Tomato-Onion Sauce
by Chef Scott Peacock, raised in Hartford

1½ pounds collard greens

6 cups smoked pork stock

⅓ cup olive oil

1 large onion, chopped (about 1¼ cups)

1 tablespoon minced garlic

½ teaspoon crushed red pepper flakes (more or less, according to taste)

Salt and freshly ground pepper to taste

1 (38-ounce) can whole, peeled tomatoes, drained

Wash and drain the collards. Remove the stems, beginning at the base of the leaf, and discard. Cut the leaves crosswise into 1-inch strips. Bring the pork stock or water to a rolling boil in a large Dutch oven, drop in the collard greens, and cook, uncovered, for 30 to 40 minutes until tender. Drain the greens and reserve the cooking liquid.

Heat the olive oil in a large skillet or Dutch oven. Add the onions and cook, stirring often, over moderate heat for 10 minutes until the pieces are translucent and tender. Add the garlic and crushed red pepper, ½ teaspoon of salt, and ½ teaspoon of freshly ground black pepper. Stir well to distribute the seasonings and cook for an additional 5 minutes. Add the drained tomatoes and 1½ cups of the liquid reserved from cooking the greens. Simmer gently for 15 minutes. Taste for seasoning and adjust as needed. Add the drained collards and simmer for an additional 10 minutes. Taste for seasoning again and serve hot.

First published in *The Gift of Southern Cooking: Recipes and Revelations from Two Great Southern Cooks,* by Edna Lewis and Scott Peacock (New York: Alfred A. Knopf, 2003). Used by permission.

Arkansas

Spicy Collards by Michael Roberts of Benton

"If using homegrown greens in this recipe, be sure to change the water a couple of times when you first start boiling them to remove any dirt. You can substitute ham hock, salt pork, or even bacon grease for pigs' feet. I choose to use pigs' feet because they have an excellent balance of meat, fat, and bone—all the things needed to make a good, rich pot liquor."

1 to 2 big bunches of greens (collards, turnip, or mustard)

1 to 2 pigs' trotters

1 onion, chopped

1 to 4 cloves garlic, chopped

2 fresh jalapeno peppers, tops cut off, left whole

½ cup distilled vinegar

Salt and pepper to taste

Add all ingredients except the vinegar to a large kettle. Cover with water and bring to a boil; reduce heat to a slow simmer. Simmering is important because it allows the trotters to release their good flavor without overcooking the greens. Once you have a good pot liquor going (meaning some of the fat has rendered into the water), add your vinegar—this helps counterbalance the bitterness of the greens and will help release the flavor of the peppers. I view vinegar as more of a spice than as a condiment because adding some acidic flavor to a dish can brighten and enhance the flavor without ever imparting sourness.

Cooking time is your choice, but I wouldn't go any less than 2 hours. Taste your greens as they cook—you're looking for the perfect balance of rich, subtle bitterness, savory pork, onion goodness, and a bit of bright spice from the peppers, garlic, and vinegar. You can remove the pig's trotters and pick the meat from it, returning the pork bits to the pot. Retain the liquid the greens cooked in—this rich broth is perfect for pouring over cornbread or peas and can make an interesting flavor addition to vegetable soup.

FLORIDA

Collard and Ham Soup by Mary Martin of Ponce de Leon

1 large onion

3 tablespoon butter

3 cups finely chopped collards

1 medium potato, diced

½ cup ham, diced

2 bouillon cubes

½ teaspoon salt

¼ teaspoon pepper

1 clove garlic

4 cups hot water

½ cup milk

Croutons (optional)

Parmesan cheese (optional)

Sauté onion and butter in large Dutch oven. Add next 8 ingredients and bring to boil. Cover and reduce heat; simmer 15 minutes until potatoes are tender. Add milk; cover and cook over low heat. Stir until heated. Ladle into bowls; you may add croutons and sprinkle with cheese.

LOUISIANA

Red River Gumbo by Mary Cheatham of Ruston

"Tasso is a peppered cut of pork used in Cajun foods. I recommend Richard's®."

1 cup small red beans

⅓ cup all purpose flour

⅓ cup olive oil

1 cup chopped onion

1 cup chopped green bell pepper

1 cup chopped celery

4 cups finely chopped fresh collards

6 ounces tasso, finely chopped

1 can diced tomatoes with green chilies

2 cups cooked, diced pork, or other meat of choice

2 tablespoons chili powder

¼ cup lemon juice

1 pound crawfish tails

2 tablespoons butter

2 cups frozen mixture of okra, tomatoes, and onions

Salt and ground pepper to taste

Gumbo filé

Cooked rice

Soak the beans overnight. Empty the water and cover again with fresh water; cook until tender.

Make a roux in the Dutch oven by browning the flour in the oil. Add the onion, bell pepper, celery, collards, and tasso. Stir and continue to heat. Add enough warm water to cover the mixture as it continues to cook. Add the tomatoes, pork, chili powder, lemon juice, and cooked red beans; keep the pot simmering. Add water as needed.

Sauté the crawfish tails in butter until they are warmed throughout.

After the gumbo has cooked until the vegetables are slightly tender, combine the okra-tomato mixture and crawfish. Adjust the seasonings by adding salt and red pepper as desired. Simmer until all the ingredients are warmed throughout. Sprinkle with gumbo filé. Serve over rice.

North Carolina

Classic East Carolina Collards by Stacy Gaskins of Ayden

3 quarts water

1 ham hock or 1 tablespoon bacon grease

Salt and pepper to taste

2 pounds collards

Use a 5-quart pot (or you won't get good collards because they'll boil over) and add water, ham hock, salt, and pepper (avoid too much salt). One of my grandmothers would add bacon grease if she didn't have meat.

Bring water to a boil while you prepare the collards.

Clean collards by removing the leaves from the stem, throwing away the outside leaves. I like to cut the stems out with a knife and remove bad spots. Fill kitchen sink with water and soak the leaves and swish to remove dirt and bugs. Rip the leaves in to 2- to 4-inch pieces. One of my grandmothers would not rip but rolled them to stick them into the pot. Add leaves to pot, making sure there's enough water to have an inch or two above the leaves. Bring back to a heavy boil and then cook on medium or medium low for 3 to 4 hours. With slotted spoon, flip the collards regularly. The top leaves don't get the heat. It's not that they stink, but the smell is not as good as the flavor. My grandmother leaves the top off—"you want that aroma"—but I leave it cracked open. Lift pot and pour into colander in sink. Use a small plate to push down on the collards, pressing water through the colander.

Put in pan or bowl and then use the collard chopper (a utensil with circular blade with jagged edges, also called a tooth-edged circular chopper—it can be purchased online).

South Carolina

Wisacky Sweet Pickle Collards by Reanell Bradley of Wisacky

1 piece of fatback or 1 ham hock

1 bunch collards (this is typically about 2 pounds)

2 cups water

Pinch of baking soda

Salt and pepper to taste

1 tablespoon sugar

Pinch of butter

Sweet pickles

Boil fatback or ham hock separately until tender. Wash and clean the collard leaves. Chop them fine; you don't want them too "stemmy."

Put 2 cups water in a large pot; you can add more later if needed. Add a pinch of baking soda and bring to a boil. Add salt and pepper to taste. Add 1 tablespoon sugar and a pinch of butter. Add the fatback or ham hock to the pot with its juice. Add the collard leaves. Boil for 20 to 25 minutes if there has been a good frost; if not, you need to cook a little longer. You don't want to get collards too mushy. Use a slotted spoon to lift collards from the pot and put in a bowl. Don't add more salt or spices at this point.

Serve collards with cornbread and sweet pickles.

4

Growing Collards
Is Broccoli Really the Same Species?

Millions of people far from the South have heard of the collard patch because of novelist Harper Lee of Monroeville, Alabama. Her best-selling book, *To Kill a Mockingbird*, is standard reading for schoolchildren all over the world. In fact, the story of Scout and her heroic father, attorney Atticus Finch, is one of the most widely read books among children and young adults. It won the Pulitzer Prize for Fiction in 1961 and has been published in more than 40 languages, with more than 30 million copies in print. The movie version is considered one of the greatest films of the sixties. Lee makes several references to collards in the book, the first of which is: "Early one morning as we were beginning our day's play in the back yard, Jem and I heard something next door in Miss Rachel Haverford's collard patch. We went to the wire fence to see if there was a puppy—Miss Rachel's rat terrier was expecting—instead we found someone sitting looking at us. Sitting down, he wasn't much higher than the collards."[1] That someone was, of course, Dill, and in Harper's story, the collard patch is visited again in the book as the children seek to know the mystery of a strange man named Boo. The patch serves as a kind of meeting ground, a place where young

Scout and her brother begin to encounter a truth about life itself: prejudices abound, but whether you are a human or a bird, and whatever your color, you are one of God's creatures and deserving of respect.

This chapter focuses on collard growing in the South, as well as on the collard in the traditional southern landscape. During our years of field work, we encountered collards growing not just in the typical small garden, but also as ornamentals on porches, as six-foot-tall shrubs, in ragged clumps by the edge of a wood, in the shade of umbrellas to prevent sun damage, and by the thousands in perfectly straight rows set by a large tractor.

DISTINGUISHING THE LEAFY GREENS

To recognize the different greens in their plant form, one must have seen them in gardens or on farms. Figure 7 shows comparative leaves of spinach, kale, collard, mustard, and turnip greens. Not only are the collard plant's leaves larger than the others, but also the plant generally grows taller, in some cases reaching over four feet when mature, while adult turnip plants will be only two feet tall, and mustard plants will reach one foot at most. The color of each of these varies, with collard leaf color varying the most due to both human breeding and natural selection.

How do these plants really differ? The answer lies in taxonomy, the science of categorizing, relating, and naming organisms. Using the common name of any organism (e.g., the collard) often leads to mistaken identity. Calling a yam a sweet potato does not make it one; they are distinct plants, the sweet potato coming from South America and the yam having been domesticated in the Old World in numerous areas of Africa and Asia. Although the plants and their tubers have similar appearances, they are not even in the same plant family. Now that DNA analysis can point to a deeper scientific understanding of the evolution of organisms, many plants that look alike are discovered to be unrelated.

And many plants that do *not* look alike are, in fact, the same species. The most extreme example of this latter situation may be *Brassica oleracea*, the scientific name for collards. *Brassica* is the genus name, a broad category that includes six related species, with these common names for their garden varieties:

- *Brassica rapa* (turnip, Chinese cabbage)
- *Brassica nigra* (black mustard, the source of the yellowish condiment)
- *Brassica carinata* (Abyssinian mustard—its seeds are the source for cooking oil in Egypt)
- *Brassica juncea* (mustard—including mustard greens)
- *Brasscia napus* (rapeseed, canola, rutabaga)
- *Brassica oleracea* (collards, cabbage, broccoli, cauliflower, kale, Brussels sprouts, and kohlrabi)

Yes, that's right. This last species is one of agriculture's most versatile vegetables, having been "domesticated" over the centuries into seven different forms. These seven vegetables are physically and gastronomically distinct enough that many people will enjoy eating one and despise another, even though they are all the same species—just as different breeds of dogs are all the same species.

The Main Enemy of a Greens Garden

Gardeners know they are outnumbered by millions of plant-chewing insects. The imported cabbage worm (*Pieris rapae*), for example, once limited to Europe and the Mediterranean, is now a major pest around the world, including in the American South. It has developed a color and texture that perfectly match the underside of this plant's leaves. The larvae/caterpillar clings tightly along the principal veins of a leaf so that it is particularly hard to see. This caterpillar metamorphoses into a moth that can lay enough eggs to destroy an entire garden of greens within a week. A prime reason to grow greens in fall and winter, then, is that fewer insects are able to damage the crop. In November, December, and January, green gardens bursting with collards, turnips, and mustard—even cabbage, kale, or broccoli—stand out against the normally brown winter landscape. All over the American South, the green patches denote a gardener who treasures *Brassica oleacea*.

SEED RETAILERS

One way to learn about the gardening of collard greens is to ask seed retailers, ranging from Kmart to farm cooperatives to hardware stores to nurseries. Some rural areas still have a seed retailer selling garden seed in bulk. Customers may request seeds of various quantities, from a quarter ounce up to a pound or more. This old-fashioned, time-honored profile doesn't fit the modern approach to retail, which employs prepackaged seed in brightly colored envelopes, marketed in shiny display racks that seem to promise postcard-perfect produce with minimal effort. The retailer has provided a convenience for not only the customer but also the cashier, the latter of whom has to simply scan the packet's bar code. No knowledge of the seed is needed, and all useful information about planting and caring for the seed is reduced to a few lines on the back of the packet. In modern retail, person-to-person communication is nearly eliminated.

Yet there are a few places operating outside this trend. In Henry's Feed & Farm Supply in tiny Whitwell, Tennessee, not far from Chattanooga, the friendly owner, when asked which greens seed sold best in his store, pulled out five-pound paper bags in which bulk seeds arrive from the supplier. He had bags labeled "purple top turnip," "curly mustard," "tender green mustard," and "Georgia collard." With what looked like a wooden flour scoop, he swirled the seed around in the bags and said, "We sell mainly turnip seed, and that's maybe 85 percent of the greens seed we sell. Mustard and collard seed don't sell so good, either one" (see fig. 8).

In order to get a better sense of seed sales in Tennessee, in 2006 and 2007 we conducted a phone survey of seed retailers, such as Henry's Feed & Farm (see table 3). A sample of retailers from forty-three different counties, out of the state's ninety-five, were asked, "Which kind of greens seed sells best?" At thirty-three of these retailers, the number one selling green was turnip, almost always the purple top variety. The other ten retailers said that mustard greens were their leading green seed. At none of the stores were collards number one, and only one retailer, in Washington County, in Northeast Tennessee, listed collards as number two. In fact, seed for kale, generally not popular in the South, was mentioned more often than collard seed (fourteen counties versus nine), although it never sold better than turnip seed and usually ranked behind mustard seed.

This data supports our field observations that Tennessee is primarily a turnip greens state. Many gardeners will mix their seed and grow mustard and turnip greens together. In perhaps a dozen Tennessee counties, kale is as popular as collards but still less popular than turnips and mustard. There was no clear geographic pattern for greens within the state.

TABLE 3. SEED SALES FOR GREENS, JULY THROUGH OCTOBER 2006, AT A WHITWELL, TENNESSEE, SEED RETAILER*

Type of Seed	Ounces Sold
Turnip, Seventop	2018
Rape (Canola)	696
Mustard, Florida Broadleaf	444
Mustard, Curly	373
Kale	319
Collard	177

*Data provided by Bedford-Moore Farmers Cooperative.

One unusual kind of greens showed up in the survey—known as "creasy greens"—in rural, mountainous Johnson County (population about 18,000) in the far northeastern corner of Tennessee, wedged between North Carolina and Virginia. Its biggest town and county seat is Mountain City, with fewer than three thousand people. This Appalachian county is the only county in a survey of several states where the retailer mentioned selling seed for creasy greens, second only to mustard greens.

Creasy greens, sometimes called greasy greens, are a lesser-known, small-leaved green (a type of cress, *Barbarea verna*, but not watercress), which was introduced long ago from Europe and now thrives on roadsides and abandoned areas of the eastern United States. Because it is the earliest of spring greens, many rural folk still go out to gather it as a ritual in March or April, depending on latitude and altitude. In many grocery stores in Appalachia, one can find canned creasy greens on the shelves and sometimes fresh creasy greens in the produce section. These greens are somewhat peppery and have a slightly bitter aftertaste. This kind of greens is little known in urban areas; indeed the name "creasy greens" may not help its popularity in new markets.

Rape is a globally important plant related to collards and cabbage. Under the name "canola," it is the third leading source of vegetable oil. Seed retailers report an interesting use for rape and sometimes for collard, turnip, and kale: feed plots to attract white-tailed deer. These graceful browsers are no longer constrained by historic predators, such as mountain lions and red wolves, and are becoming garden pests in many areas of the country where they can completely consume a garden of greens. In fact, some wildlife managers will plant feed plots of Brassica plants to reduce the deer damage on native forest vegetation. Since collards and other Brassicas remain green in winter, even under snow, deer will browse the leaves, finding good nutrition in a time of scarcity. Hunters can plant small feed plots in secluded areas of the woods where deer may feel comfortable feeding by daylight, which is the legal time to shoot them. So, if one comes across a small clearing planted with collards, rape, or turnips while walking in a forest in November or December, be sure to don a blaze orange hunting-safety hat!

Although seed sales are indicative of what is grown in an area's gardens, most typical gardeners simply buy their plants, as Mattie Brown does in Mound Bayou, Mississippi (see fig. 10). She is a widow, with "a little money and a whole lot of arthritis." "It's hard for me to get the seed to do what I want, so my friend gets the seedlings in Clarksdale for me," she said. Unlike some gardeners, she did not keep track of the variety. She waters and weeds them, though, to make sure she has a good supply of greens all winter. "I figure I spend about eight dollars in September, and I eat off that for months."

The largest wholesaler of collard seedlings in the country—well, the world, actually—is located just 20 miles south of Tuskegee, Alabama. In a typical year, Bonnie Plants ships some eight million collard seedlings to retailers all over the South. The company's president, Stan Copes, states, "My grandparents started farming in 1917, selling cabbage, and then they gradually shifted to selling other plants." They added collards to their product line in the thirties and now have growing facilities all over the United States and contracts with nearly all the major garden retailers. "Our best sales are at stores in rural areas, since that's where people have larger gardens," he says.

Bonnie Plants does most of its seedling growing in greenhouses. Plants leave these hothouses in excellent condition, but a good percentage, perhaps forty percent, don't make it to someone's garden. "That's because some won't be bought in time," he said. "The collard seedling's shelf life ranges from a few days to two weeks, but all depends on the staff in the stores, who may forget to water them. It's not their priority, usually." The collard, like any garden plant, will always retain a delicacy that mocks the modern world's industrialization of our food system.

From a mail survey sent to agricultural extension agents, more geographic detail emerged of where collard gardens are most common. The survey asked the following questions: Are collards widely grown in your county? Is the collard patch the most important winter garden activity in your area, and, if not, what garden activity is more common? If collards are grown in your area, have you noticed a decrease or increase in their production over the past few years, and, if so, what reasons might explain this change? Are there commercial collard growers (even small ones) in your area?

The results indicated relatively fewer collard gardens situated in metropolitan areas throughout the South. Why is gardening of vegetables generally less common in cities and suburbs? We believe that at least the following four factors are involved.

First, many subdivisions exclude them, either by regulation or social pressure. Vegetable gardens are perceived as "working landscape features," much like clotheslines and work sheds, and the yards in most modern suburbs, with their unused lawns and ornamental plantings, are designed to demonstrate a leisurely lifestyle. Vegetable gardens, for many urbanites and suburbanites, are not allowed, out of fear that they will lower property values. Some people erect fences designed to screen their backyard, and behind such a fence could lurk a greens garden.

Second, in densely settled areas, garden space is often unavailable or impractical. For example, in Cammack Village, a small suburb (population 831) just west of Little Rock, Arkansas, there are more than three hundred house lots that are only sixty by one-hundred twenty feet, and nearly every square foot not covered by a house is shaded by trees. There are no gardens. In a long, hot summer, that shade surely makes those homes much more comfortable. What Southerner does not cherish shade? Even though our investigations uncovered quite a few urban gardens and even commercial production within cities, these were exceptions, due partly to the constraints of space and the need to maximize the utility of expensive urban land.

Third, indoor comforts and distractions have multiplied dramatically since World War II. Air conditioning, central heating, television, home computers, video games, and the internet comprise the convenience lifestyle that holds us indoors, more and more. Psychological research shows that once people find all their comforts entirely inside the home, they begin to feel rather uncomfortable outside.[2] Quite a few interviewees said they quit keeping a garden because of one of the natural elements: heat, cold, drought, or insects. Why go outside and deal with these—and even dangerous ultraviolet radiation—when you can be more comfortable indoors?

Finally, it seems that urban and suburban residents are more likely to eat at restaurants and buy prepared foods for home consumption and less likely to follow the rural traditions of growing one's own food. Indeed, we found out that more than half the meals eaten in Arkansas are eaten away from home. Fast food is, for many rural people, their one taste of the city life. This "urban" lifestyle is simply more commoditized: you buy what you need. Urban and even suburban people seem to eat greens less often. Except for barbeque, the "country foods" seem to be partially displaced by a more cosmopolitan cuisine, perhaps simply through constant exposure to different cultures or through an effort to avoid being stigmatized as rural or poor. Thankfully, there are many exceptions to this trend.

It appears that many rural Southern families raised a winter collard patch during much of the twentieth century. An example in Plains, Georgia, may be expected to continue far into the future. At the boyhood home of former president Jimmy Carter, the National Park Service grows collards. You can see them every fall and winter, cultivated just as they were when Carter was growing up. The grounds manager says that the former president personally makes sure that heirloom collards are grown from saved seed, just as they were in his childhood. This choice of greens is made consciously: writing about his childhood on a farm in Southern Georgia, Carter says that during his youth in the 1930s, his family ate turnips and cabbage, but their favorite greens were collards.[3] The Park Service's garden produce is now donated to a local food bank.

Today, even in many rural areas, small kitchen gardens are scarce. In eastern Arkansas, on the Mississippi delta, a floodplain with vast and startlingly flat monoculture farms, homes and even trees are uncommon, and hypnotizing rows of soybeans and cotton extend to the hazy horizon. This is technically "rural" country, but there are few small farms. Arkansas's many large rice farms are evident (this state produces about 40 percent of the country's rice crop), but most homes (and, thus, people) were removed from this landscape as fields were consolidated into corporate farms comprised of thousands of acres. There are few home gardens, even where the descendants of tenant farmers, or recently arrived farm laborers, have plenty of space for them.

In the days of tenant farming, there may have also been few gardens in the delta. Landowners may not have allowed them, as they squeezed the maximum cash crop production out of the land. Here's what one African American tenant farmer from Holly Grove, Mississippi, in Monroe County, said on the subject in 1939: "The landlord wouldn't give us no land for a garden, or no wire to fence it, if we could of got some land. He ain't like Mister Brewer down the road. Mister Brewer gives his 'croppers land for a garden, and if they use it he don't charge no rent, but if they don't use it he makes 'em pay rent on it, eight dollars an acre—but we had to plant cotton right up to the door."[4] Since all landowners wouldn't have been so harshly "efficient" as the first landowner, it is likely that patches of leafy greens were found all around rural Arkansas, for we found quite a few historical references to collards and turnips. For example, in 1936, Samuel Taylor, a former slave from Clark County, Arkansas, recalled his family having a small garden with turnips and collards on a plantation before emancipation.[5] Another former slave said that when he was young and living in Hempstead County he regularly ate collards and turnips from the garden beside their cabin.[6] Adolphus James Boyd of Pulaski County kept a journal through 1911 in which he recorded all his gardening activity. On April 22, he planted collards; the next week he planted turnips.

Keeping a collard patch seems to have been a tradition among many but not all rural folks. A 1974 article about the "Cajun" minority in Washington County, Alabama, quotes a local as saying, "Have you noticed that none of the [Cajun people's] houses have gardens around them? . . . A colored person will have a little garden with a few collards, if nothing else."[7]

ARE HOME GARDENS DISAPPEARING FROM THE LANDSCAPE?

A Harris Poll taken from 1995 to 2004 asked people around the United States to choose their favorite leisure activities from a supplied list. It found that the proportion of respondents choosing gardening as a leisure activity dropped in those ten years from nine percent to six percent. It is possible that gardening is not considered a "leisure" activity by many, as it requires physical activity and a bit of sweat equity.

Later, a sequence of polls by the National Gardening Association showed an apparent turnaround in this trend. With a definition of food gardening including vegetables, berries, fruit, and herbs, that data estimated that, between 2004 and 2005, the number of households with some kind of home garden rose from twenty-four to twenty-seven million.[8] Then, in 2010, the poll actually showed a remarkable 22 percent increase over 2009 in the time people spent food gardening. The survey concluded that the number of households participating in food gardening rose that year by 14 percent, from thirty-six million households to forty-one million. These national surveys show a recent increase in home gardens, possibly related to the financial recession that began in 2007 to 2008, the worst downturn since the Great Depression. An increase in do-it-yourself activities, such as home gardening, could also be attributed to the rise in popularity of the "local food" movement. Even as just a minor player in this food movement, collards may have a brighter outlook.

SURVEY OF FAMILY GARDENING PATTERNS

It is common lore that the American landscape prior to 1945 was one in which the vast majority of rural families grew a kitchen garden. As part of the 2007 college student survey, a more scientific assessment of home gardening over recent decades has emerged. This survey of 12,611 students at community and four-year colleges, located in the ten-state study area, should be fairly representative of the status quo[9] (see table 4).

Table 4. State-by-State Survey Results of College Students When Asked Two Questions:

(1) Do or did your grandparents regularly have a vegetable garden?

(2) Does your family now have a vegetable garden?

State	% Yes & Yes	% Yes & No	% No & No
Alabama	27.3	61.4	9.6
Arkansas	31.1	58.5	8.9
Florida	20.8	52.8	24.9
Georgia	27.5	50.4	22.1
Louisiana	27.3	55.2	16.9
Mississippi	32.9	54.5	11.2
North Carolina	36.5	50.8	11.3
South Carolina	30.5	50.6	18.9
Tennessee	33.6	54.1	11.3
Virginia	34.9	51.8	13.3
Total	31.7	53.4	14

Total Surveyed	Total Yes & Yes	Total Yes & No	Total No & No
1172	320	724	112
212	66	124	19
197	41	104	49
2010	553	1013	444
1086	297	600	184
2183	719	1190	245
2788	1017	1416	315
684	209	346	129
1431	481	774	162
848	297	441	110
12611	4000	6732	1769

Note: There were so few "No & Yes" answers (that is, "my grandparents never had a vegetable garden, but my family now does have one")—well under 1%—that those responses were not tabulated here.

Viewing the South as a whole, about 85 percent of students surveyed (the sum of the first and second columns) say their grandparents do or did keep a vegetable garden. This result is in keeping with the general assumption that the vast majority of Americans (and particularly southerners) were gardening around 1955. Interviewees support this notion. A 1942 study of family food habits in Alabama found that 71 percent of families kept a home vegetable garden.[10] But, by 2007, only 32 percent of surveyed students said their parents had a garden. It is clear that certain states have seen a greater change than others. Arkansas respondents presented a startling change: 90 percent say their grandparents keep or kept a garden, but now only 31 percent of their parents do, a decline of nearly 60 percent. North Carolina appears to have maintained the highest rate of current home gardening, with 36.5 percent. The more urbanized state of Florida has the lowest current rate, with 20.8 percent. Even in Florida in the 1950s, however, most families (73 percent) had a garden. So, in the past fifty years or so, gardening has dropped from a major landscape feature to an uncommon one in much of the study area. A profound shift has occurred in the Southern landscape.

ATLANTA'S URBAN GARDENING PROGRAM

Thankfully, the recent past is still alive in our elders, who have gardening skills and experience. Helen Mason, age 78, lives in a public housing facility in Atlanta. "I grew up a few miles from Covington, Georgia, and we had a big garden, more than half an acre. I started gardening when I was about nine, following my mother along. She had a walking cane, and she would walk along making holes and I would put the seed in there and cover it up. When I was grown up tall, I did the same thing. I've got a cane for the garden, and I walk along and punch a hole and drop the seed in. Then when I had children, I taught them all about the garden—how to weed it out. Daddy plowed it with a mule. But then my parents and my husband and I moved to Atlanta in 1961 and we just didn't have room to plant a garden anymore. It was many years later, in 1993, when I moved into this housing facility, and I was still missing the garden.

"Then in 1997 Bobby Wilson showed up, bringing the Atlanta Urban Gardening Program, a project of the University of Georgia's agricultural extension office. We were so happy when we got our community garden (located on a gentle slope in the housing project 100 by 40 feet). Nearly every day in the warm season I go out there. I'll go out early in the morning, work about three hours, stop working in the middle part of the day, then go back in the evening and work three more hours. Some days I might work all day, maybe twelve hours, because the garden needs watering, and I'll be out there 'til nine o'clock at night" (see fig. 9).

Mason continues, "Lots of times the gardeners talk to each other. Sometimes people are sharing their knowledge about how to garden. Someone may ask me how I got my plants to grow so well, and I'm happy to show them. I like to grow things that look pretty. So I grow collards, cabbage, broccoli, green beans, running pole beans, squash, corn, sweet potato, peanuts . . . Carrots are pretty too, but they're too slow. I'll grow the purple-top turnip, and the rape. I plant seeds in those little cups, and people can come to me for their plants and not have to go to the store.

"For collards, sometimes I'll plant in March to have an early garden, but mostly they're for the fall. So I plant them in the last of July or the start of August. What we do is plant the seed mostly, instead of the little plants, because with seed you know what you got. I like the Georgia collards. They'll last you all winter. Now it used to be in the late fall you'd have some pretty greens, but lately some bugs have just come out of nowhere.

"I had my heart attack not long ago, and they told me I'd never garden again. That was like cutting my *legs* off. I had nobody to look after my garden, so it was just taken up with weeds, and I just sat in the window upstairs and looked and looked. For a year my garden was just disappearing. It was breaking my heart. But then I got where I could get out again. You *have* to, 'cause whatever problems you got, all the stress and anything that's on your mind, working in that garden will get rid of it. You don't need to go anywhere else to get help. It's therapy. Back in the early spring I burned my hand on the stove and had a cast on it, but that didn't stop me. I still set out my collard and cabbage plants. I'll surprise my family. Last year I grew all this sweet corn and didn't tell them, and I shelled it and cooked it up and they tasted it and said 'This tastes like *garden* corn,' and I said, 'that's because it *is*.'"

Because her garden has been central to her life, Mason has spoken out publicly to try to keep funding for Atlanta's Urban Gardening Program. "I had never been up in front of important people before, but I went and spoke to the county commission. Right before my turn, the fellow turned and said I had only two minutes! Good Lord, what can you say in two minutes? I was so shocked I had trouble getting the words out." Wilson pitched in at this point and said, "She still did well. In her very genteel way, she made her point. We got the funding." Then Mason added, "And my brother saw me on television." The gardeners seem to count on the stability of the staff in this program knowing they can have faith in Bobby and Cathy (Walker, another extension agent). "We're like their coaches, and we are going to stick by them," said Wilson. "There is a real loyalty between these gardeners and us."

Mason has hundreds of photos of the gardens her community has grown over the years: photos of huge and well-tended collards, okra, cabbages, broccoli, tomatoes, gourds, peanuts, sweet corn, sweet potatoes, pole beans, squash, peppers, and many kinds of flowers as well. As she narrated the photos, she named all the different gardeners who worked with her. There is a powerful beauty in these plants, according to Mason: every plant reminds her of her friends, some long gone, but also the hard work and pains she has endured. With her example, it is easy to imagine how much better public housing could be if gardens were central to their design, as they are in Atlanta.

Mason's story is like that of many apartment dwellers, condominium owners, even suburbanites who want to garden in an urbanizing South. Persistent gardening advocates, such as Bobby Wilson, have backed similar campaigns in many cities. The leading proponent of urban community gardens is the American Community Gardening Association (www.

communitygarden.org). The Atlanta Urban Gardening Program is one of the most successful, having helped create and maintain about two hundred community gardens around Atlanta, mostly in low- and mixed-income neighborhoods, all of which nurture collards.

FARMS AND GARDENS—HOW MANY ARE THERE?

Collards are a southern tradition, but from a national perspective, they are merely one of a broader category of greens, making up only a small part of the country's total vegetable production. The 2012 Census of Agriculture indicated that collards were the leading *Brassica* green at the national level (see table 5).

TABLE 5. NATIONAL PRODUCTION OF BRASSICA GREENS BY ACRES HARVESTED*

Type of Greens	Acres Harvested
Collard	12,542
Turnip	7,070
Mustard	6,925
Kale	6,256

*2012 Census of Agriculture

To put those acreages in perspective, consider that in the same year US farmers harvested 4.5 million acres of vegetables, and plenty of other vegetables had much higher numbers than collards, such as those in table 6.

Table 6. Harvested Acres of Various Popular Vegetables in the United States*

Vegetable	Acreage Harvested
Broccoli	128,938
Cabbage	66,035
Spinach	46,377
Cauliflower	42,082
Green peas	21,942

*2012 Census of Agriculture

But some other well-known vegetables had less acreage devoted to them than collards, such as those in table 7.

Table 7. Harvested Acres of Various Other Popular Vegetables in the United States*

Vegetable	Acreage Harvested
Artichokes	7,339
Brussels sprouts	7,589
Eggplant	5,004
Okra	2,377

*2012 Census of Agriculture

This census data reports only the *commercial* production of vegetables. It likely misses a significant number of the smallest-scale commercial growers, from pick-your-own places to diversified family farms that sell locally. And there is no data on home garden production, which would add quite a few acres over the region. For instance, if only one out of fifty southern households has a collard patch each year in the ten states of the study area (27.8 million households), there would be 556,000 collard patches. If each averaged 16 square yards in area—enough space for 12 to 20 plants—that would mean about 1,838 acres of collards, and these patches would be absent from the census. If this estimate is accepted, then the total collard production in the South is 16 percent higher than the farm census indicates.

The geography of collard greens is also discovered in many unusual places as well as those not covered by the census, such as the Mississippi Department of Corrections, where several large farms produce corn, collards, and other vegetables for correctional institutions throughout the state. The 25,000 men and women held in correctional facilities around Mississippi are eating about half a pound of greens per week.

Prison farm production matches other data on Mississippi regarding the popularity of the different kinds of greens: for 2001 (the most recent year for which data are available), 121,000 pounds of collard greens, valued at $40 thousand, were produced, while there were 141,810 pounds of mustard greens, valued at $44 thousand, and 588,470 pounds of turnip greens (by far the highest), valued at $194 thousand.

In Alabama, the state penitentiary in Limestone County, just south of the Tennessee line, maintains one of the state's largest collard farms. Inmates there work on the prison farm to provide fresh produce for the facility's kitchen. The single year 2005 yielded 20,870 pounds of corn, 27,400 pounds of cabbage, 13,530 pounds of collards, 8,260 pounds of squash, 990 pounds of onions, and 500 pounds of cucumbers, making this one of the largest vegetable farms in the state. It is interesting to note that no greens other than collards were grown. Compared with Mississippi, where the prisoners grow all three kinds of greens and collards come in third, Alabama *does* seem to be more of a collard state.

A review of the historical record confirms that collards have been growing in Alabama for a long time. The following sources help to interpret past foodways:

> In late October 1813, during the Creek War, a soldier named Beard left the safety of Fort Madison (in what is now Clarke County) to gather a supply of potatoes and collards for the stockade. Beard was busy picking collards from a patch when, according to a witness, he was attacked by several Indians who killed and scalped him.[11]

> In 1833, an Alabama farmer wrote a letter to the editor of the Richmond, Virginia, *Farmer's Register* describing the "backwardness" of agriculturists in his home state, stating, "They cultivate cotton and corn, Irish potatoes and long 'collards,' just as they did as long ago as my recollection extends."[12]

> In 1853, after having toured Alabama, horticulturist C. A. Peabody complained that this scene was "far too common": "A house, with a garden of 60 feet by 40 feet in its rear, full of long collards (fit only for cows and then when steamed), the oaks cut down in front, a Spanish mulberry or China tree planted in their stead, under the shade of which is seen in the summer time a lazy pack of egg-sucking hounds."[13]

Home vegetable gardening has faded from the lives of most Americans, but it may be revived by the education of young people. In the charming small town of Greensboro, Alabama, the local elementary school was host to a large experiment in gardening in fall 2010: in August they planted a section of the playground with 900 collard seedlings. By November they were able to harvest and either sell or give away hundreds of pounds of the greens. Given the recent awareness of high childhood obesity and diabetes rates, the program was built on the hope that the children's "investment" in growing the greens would increase their openness to making the consumption of leafy greens a regular habit.

Selling Collards

When Leafy Greens Mean Money

The New Year's Day tradition of eating collards and black-eyed peas is said to derive from the notion that eating foods that look like money (dollar bills and pennies) may help bring riches in the coming year. In fact, one upscale supermarket in Virginia was found to offer a prepackaged "New Year's Salad," containing shredded raw collards, black-eyed peas, roasted tomatoes, parsley, and Italian herbs for the high price of $7.99 a pound! So, collards can represent money and are, in fact, becoming more and more commercialized as they are converted into a commodity. As the entire world sees a gradual shift away from rural culture, fewer individuals are directly involved in gardening and food production for subsistence. The local collard landscape of the American South has been fading from many areas, only to expand into a few large-scale farms growing and selling commercialized collards.

GROCERY STORES

At a small, pleasant local grocery named Harvest Foods in De Queen, Arkansas, the shift manager, a fairly young man in his late twenties, was asked, "Which greens sell best in your store?" He said without pause, "Turnip greens. After that, mustard. And after that, collard."

In exploring southern food traditions, supermarket produce sections can be fine places to learn about local culture. Produce managers are gold mines of information on what and how local people eat. These managers are usually well informed because they track what sells and are whom customers come to to ask questions and even make specific requests. Regular customers will sometimes make friends with a produce manager at a chain supermarket in the same manner as they would a neighborhood grocer who makes direct decisions about what goes on the shelves, not controlled by far-off central offices.

In Evergreen, Alabama, the Super Giant grocery store, in spite of its name, is a small store compared with those of major chains but carries a large selection of produce. The department is run by a man in his twenties, who told us that collards are his best-selling green by far, with turnip and mustard in second and third places. In his words: "We keep the fresh collards looking good by careful handling, and they'll last three days on the shelf before they wilt too much to sell. People call to see if the collard truck is in—they'll time their shopping to that. We try to remember to take the collards into the cooler at night: We soak them in lukewarm water for 5 to 10 minutes, dry them off, and leave them in the cooler. People will buy the bagged greens, but mostly only if we don't have fresh ones." There are still a few produce managers like this man who have some independence. He or she is able to purchase produce from local growers and respond to customer preferences, and has knowledge of fruits and vegetables, such as when they're in season, what keeps them fresh, even how to prepare them.

Once there were truck gardens throughout the South, planted partly with the purpose of making some cash with the extra produce. But these are hard to find now. The store manager for the relatively small Food Tiger grocery store in Heidelberg, Mississippi, said that back in the 1970s "we would be approached every year by local producers with all kinds of vegetables to sell, including collards. You might call them farmers, but they were big-time gardeners who would grow maybe half an acre of collards. They could keep us pretty well supplied. Now I don't think there is a single local grower; no one even tries to make money in collards around here anymore. Boy, we could sell 'em if we could get 'em." In much of the South, it seems gardening for profit, like farming for a living, is altogether endangered.

Yet, there are promoters of truck farming. Take Dr. Booker T. Whatley of Tuskegee, Alabama. For him, two acres of collards were assumed to be a component of the model Southern farm. From his bully pulpit as a professor at the renowned Tuskegee Institute, he argued that a farmer could earn $100,000 on 25 acres. In the 1970s and 1980s, his model farm near Tuskegee included many vegetables and fruits, and he demonstrated that such profits ("enough for a middle-class lifestyle") were possible. In some ways, Whatley was ahead of his time: he stressed that it would be necessary to minimize labor costs by having local residents come to pick their own, a notion that was unpopular at the time. But Whatley's model has since been proven viable with the proliferation of "pick-your-own" produce farms near cities in every state.

At a beautiful direct-sales farm growing collards in southern Mississippi, on the Old River Road outside of Columbia, we met a couple of friendly farmers, Lamar and Emma Dale, working 44 acres. As they are now each over age 60, Emma said it is more of a hobby farm. They raise cattle on some of the land and plant just three acres in vegetables. Emma said that with their collards they use mostly an organic insecticide called Bt, which stands for Bacillus thuringiensis, a kind of bacterium, available in farm supply and garden stores in powder form. This bacterium produces a protein that when eaten by moths, butterflies, and beetles damages their gut and causes death. It is considered an organic pesticide because it occurs naturally in these insects, just not at toxic levels, and tests have found no ill effects on humans, other mammals, fish, or birds. Research confirmed that Bt is being used by gardeners and farmers all over the South.

Born in 1942, Emma was raised on a truck farm in North Georgia and helped her father raise turnips and other vegetables. So when she was rearing her children in Mississippi, she saw the chance to make some side money right near the house. "We started getting serious about raising vegetables in the 1980s, when I got tired of Lamar giving 'em all away. I went and rented a little building in town, and I would gather 'em, wash 'em, put 'em in the truck, and drive the five miles." Now, the Dales grow more than an acre of greens, plus about five acres of such vegetables as sweet corn and tomatoes.

Because Lamar has had heart trouble, Emma does most of the work. Their son is a teacher and helps in the summer and weekends. But they have cut back, she says, "Because we're old!" She no longer rents a building in town to sell her produce, so people have to drive out to their place to get their vegetables. "But they do come," she says, because they like fresh greens around here. Columbia, the county seat, has only about 6,600 people, so to see such demand for fresh produce is impressive.

Social security checks keep the bills paid, and their garden produce has lately been enough to keep them fed, says Emma. So why do Emma and Lamar still grow and sell the vegetables? "I enjoy foolin' with 'em. I couldn't sit on my hands. Katrina hit us bad here," she told us. "All our fences were knocked down by the trees. No power for three weeks. And our greens were just plain ruined."

She told us that mustard greens sell well before other greens are ready; she can start harvesting the leaves in late October after planting them in mid-September. Her customers show up in good numbers, asking for fresh greens from October through March. The turnips and turnip greens come in about November, and then the collards sell well around Thanksgiving, Christmas, and New Year's. The turnips and mustard don't thrive in the late winter, so that's when the collards kick in.

Although Emma and Lamar have made a steady side income on a small farm catering to local tastes and preferences, farming in the South has long been driven by what could sell well in larger, more distant markets. Non-Southerners are more likely to cook cabbage or spinach as their leafy vegetable, if indeed they have anything like greens. Ambitious commercial men have indicated that the collard as a vegetable taking up space on arable acres held the South's farmers back from their full potential. In 1831, for instance, a Georgia plantation owner wrote that "if long collards are eatable, surely large fine heads of early-York, Savoy and drum-head cabbages must be better."[1] This clear bias among elites against collards probably derives not from how they taste, but from the missed opportunity to export cabbages to northern markets (collards, being unpopular among northern city residents, have limited sales potential). The demands of commerce can very often reform rural places, changing the cultures: wherever tobacco was adopted as a cash crop in the South, smoking and chewing tobacco became more common. So where investors shift Southern market crops from collards to cabbages or other more "national" greens, a parallel switch in the local diet can occur.

FARMERS' MARKETS AND ROADSIDE STANDS

Seeking a niche in the food market, some collard farmers sell their produce in local farmers' markets. In 2014, the US Department of Agriculture reported that there were 8,144 famers' markets in the country—up from 6,132 in 2010—and the trend is still upward.[2] Among Southern states, North Carolina leads with 217 farmers' markets, Virginia has 200, Florida comes in third with 128, and Georgia is fourth with 124. In last place were Louisiana and Mississippi, with each having nearly 50 farmers' markets. If we take populations into account, Virginia and North Carolina farmers' markets are thriving, since both have over 23 markets per million residents, while Florida has fewer than seven markets per million residents.

Farmers have been growing and selling produce direct to customers since the birth of commercial agriculture. But the expansion of cities and the demand for staple grains and meats led to centuries of specialization. Most farmers with hopes of reliable profits joined the long-distance commodity market system and sold through brokers and wholesalers. Although costs of production rose with the industrial age, prices paid to farmers have been either too unpredictable or predictably low.

It is not surprising, then, to see some farmers turn or return to serving local markets directly. In fact, the local food movement has been reviving around the country since the 1990s. In many parts of the South, farmers now sell directly to local restaurants, where they find a steadier demand. One example is The Harvest Table in Meadowview, Virginia. They feature locally grown collards on their menu every now and then, when the greens are in season. The restaurant was started by Steven Hopp after the success of *Animal, Vegetable, Miracle*, the book he co-authored with his wife, Barbara Kingsolver, and daughter Camille. That chronicle of a year of eating only local food, which features buying from farmers' markets, became a *New York Times* best seller.[3]

One young farmer thriving on the "direct-to-consumer" approach is Tom Garrison, whose farm is beside Highway 76 outside of Anderson, South Carolina, near the Georgia state line. Hopping off a tractor beside a large field of collards, Tom said he manages the twenty-acre family farm, called Denver Downs Farm, for his father, Ed. The farm has been in their family since 1872. Tom has gradually phased out row crops such as soybeans and feed corn, and gone to fresh produce, which he says sells very well. His big season is the Christmas/New Year's holiday season, when he sells collards. He finds his greatest earnings come from selling directly to customers, but he also sells to a few vendors in the nearby city of Anderson.

"I spent a long time looking for my niche, trying lots of things," he said, and has placed his focus on quality. His collards are grown on organic principles (no chemical pesticides), but his farm is not certified organic because it is too expensive. He said the customers come to him for collards because they are: chemical-free, larger than those in the supermarket ("every bunch is an armload"), fresher than anywhere else, because they are cut "within hours of being sold," available in more than one variety—some people ask for a "heading collard," and planted within view of the road "where people can see them growing"

Tom shops around for his seed, since collard seeds cost $180 a pound.

"You get maybe 80,000 seeds per pound, but not all will germinate. Last year, an entire field of seed failed to germinate." The company replaced it for free, but he had lost valuable growing time. Tom normally buys one pound of "Top Bunch" plus smaller amounts of two or three other varieties, especially the old "Georgia." He grows Georgia collards for "older folks who ask for them." Sometimes Tom has trouble getting his seed. For example, last year he could not find Top Bunch, so he ending up going to South Georgia to get seedlings there. He also likes to try different varieties; he has tried "Flash," "Hi-Crop," and "Blue Max." He knows of no one saving seed; he'd be interested in seeing the yellow cabbage collard, too.

By working to secure a diverse range of buyers, some commercial growers can make a good side income on one acre. One example is David Weeks, who lives near Dunn, in eastern North Carolina. In a typical year Weeks puts out 3,500 plants and has been doing so since 1998, when he retired from driving a tractor trailer. David usually grows only cabbage collards, although some years he puts out a green cabbage collard and an old-timey yellow cabbage collard. He normally sells the mature leaves for $1.50 per bunch but may charge only $1.00 a bunch if they are small. He sells his collards in several ways: When people come to his house and field, he cuts stalks off at ground level and sells the entire plant. In late November and December, he also takes loads of collards to a site in Dunn where passing drivers can stop at his truck and buy collards by the bunch. He also sells some collards to Piggly Wiggly grocery stores in Clinton and Roseboro.

Making a significant profit from a small farm, when consumers can buy for less at a supermarket, is a challenge Tom Garrison and David Weeks share. To help bring out specialty customers, the federal government has linked farmers' markets to the Special Supplemental Nutrition Program for Women, Infants, and Children (WIC) and other food programs for lower-income citizens. For example, Alabama now distributes some $2 million in farmers' market coupons for women, children, and the elderly every year. At farmers' markets in the fall (many markets remain open until

Thanksgiving), superior fresh collards are sold at the same price as super-market collards. This is a boon to both the small farmer (since no inter-mediary agent is taking a cut of that price) and the customer (who is often buying superior produce).

ROADSIDE SALES

On a mid-December morning on the courthouse square in Abbeville, Al-abama, with sunny skies and a pleasant temperature of 60 degrees Fahr-enheit, Troy Wilson sat on the edge of a small flatbed trailer chock-full of collards. Blankets covered most of the leaves to keep the sun from drying them out, but enough were visible to allow potential customers to see them. His price was $3.00 a bundle. A middle-aged man who has sold different kinds of vegetables for much of his life, Troy began this project by "buying" a field of 8,000 collard plants from a friend. Troy and his friend timed it so that the collards would be ready for harvest in late November through late December. That's a major peak time in sales, when people serve large fam-ily feast–sized servings of collards. He says the real sales peaks are during the four days before each of the three big fall and winter holidays: Thanks-giving, Christmas, and New Year's Day.

Troy makes his best profits selling directly from his vehicle because he doesn't have to share the sales revenue, but sometimes he also sells his collards to a local grocery store, a small franchise of Giant Foods. And to improve the sales in that store, Troy now does some food processing. He sits at his kitchen table and cuts the collard leaves up, stuffing them into clear plastic bags (designed to hold ice). These bags of cut collards ordinarily sell for more than loose collards, and the customers buy them up quickly.

Troy says collards can sell better than turnip greens because they tend to look good longer after being harvested. "Turnip greens start to wilt just a few hours after you cut them. But if you have outdoor temperatures be-tween 40 and 50 degrees Fahrenheit, your collards will easily last four days after harvest."

MEDIUM-SIZED FARMS

In the hamlet of Tyler, Alabama, on a bend in the Alabama River, James Anthony Minter IV (he goes by Jay; his son goes by "Five") runs a profitable small farm. His land in the river bend was formerly a large cotton plantation with 250 sharecropper families living on it. The last of those families left in the 1950s to search for jobs when workers were replaced by cotton picking machines.

These days, like many farms around the South—especially smaller cotton and tobacco farms—the Minter farm has switched to a crop with higher returns: fresh produce. Minter says they make most of their profits by growing and processing greens, especially collards. "We converted our old cotton gin building into a processing facility." He not only processes and sells his own produce (usually about ten acres planted in collards), but also the greens from other producers. Jay's employees clean, chop, and bag the collards, and he sells these to both stores and brokers.

Locally bagged collards are becoming increasingly popular in parts of the South, since processed greens are more convenient for shoppers. In Eufaula, Alabama, locally bagged collards are sold at Piggly Wiggly. This store gets bunches of collards from a small local grower, and then several store employees process them. One of the main employees involved in this work, a young woman named Shekeena Respass, says she washes the leaves, cuts off the stems, cuts the leaves into pieces about an inch across, and stuffs them into bags in one-pound quantities. These bagged greens sell for about $1.99 a pound at a rate almost as fast as the full bunches of fresh collards priced at $2.69 a bunch.

MAJOR COMMERCIAL PRODUCTION OF COLLARDS

Further up the scale of production is the large produce farm, such as those in Georgia. America's leading commercial producer of collard, no state comes close to the total acreage Georgia has dedicated to the growing of collards (see table 8). Georgia also has the largest collard farms, on average, although none of those large farms grow solely collards. Grady County, Georgia (the county seat of which is the town of Cairo) has 930 acres devoted to collards, which surely makes it one of the country's leading producing counties. Only two other southern counties reported more acreage: Colquitt, Georgia, just northeast of Grady County, with 1,391 acres, and Lexington County, in South Carolina, with 1,744 acres, probably the number one collard county in the United States.

TABLE 8. COLLARD PRODUCTION BY US STATE*

State	Acres	Farms	Avg Farm Size
Georgia	3081	114	27.03
South Carolina	2668	114	23.4
North Carolina	2444	202	12.09
Alabama	285	107	2.66
Florida	274	117	2.34
Virginia	77	51	1.51
Mississippi	66	32	2.06
Louisiana	32	15	2.13
Arkansas	3	7	0.43
Tennessee	**	15	n.a.

*2012 Census of Agriculture

**Census Bureau reported no acreage data for Tennessee to protect the identities of the small number of producers in that state.

Tift County, Georgia, is home to what may be the second largest producer of greens in the country: the family-owned Roberson Farm. Its founder, the late Wendell Roberson, was born on this land in 1935. He built up this family business until it became one of the largest growers of leafy greens in the country. The breakthrough came in the 1960s when Wendell signed a contract to sell greens to a man named Mr. Castellini in the Cincinnati, Ohio, area. In those early days, Wendell would buy greens produced by small farmers near Tifton. He would take vanloads of workers to farms around South Georgia and northern Florida in order to harvest enough greens to fill the demand in northern states.

In the 1960s and 1970s, these field hands were virtually all African Americans. Since the 1980s, however, a steady transition has occurred so that now most of the company's 160 employees are Hispanic. In fact, since about 1986 the farm has participated in a government program called H-2A, which brings workers from Mexico on buses. These "nonimmigrant foreign workers"[4] are guaranteed a minimum wage rate and the farm provides them with free housing. Terrell Roberson said if it weren't for the Mexican workers, the farm would not have sufficient labor to operate. The company office actually has framed group photos on its walls, showing all the workers from each year, posed outside their bus. Terrell says, "They are a part of the family. They are good employees."

The Roberson farm now extends across 4,000 acres in Tift and Worth counties, 3,500 of those owned outright and 500 under lease. In a typical year about 300 acres are used for collards, 200 for turnip greens, 200 for mustard greens, 100 acres for kale, 100 acres for slick-leaf mustard, 200 for green peas, 300 for butterbeans, and 600 for peanuts (the remaining land is in forest or fallow). But the number one product of the business is collards, accomplished through multiple harvests—sometimes five harvests from the same plants (see fig. 14).

Here's the Roberson system: A farm vehicle discs a 36-inch row that it shapes into a raised bed. This device, traveling at five miles per hour, is rigged by Terrell, the eldest son. Following right behind is another piece of equipment with a vacuum pump that pulls individual seeds through a filter plate and plants the seed, about one every 24 inches and ¼ inch deep. Every month except November and December, acres of collards are planted in this way. Terrell prefers to plant the Top Bunch hybrid; it has a more upright habit than others, he says. He plants some acreage with Champion hybrid seed because this is slower to "bolt," or go to flower. But Champion's leaves tend to flop over, which creates a challenge for harvesting later on.

All the acreage planted in greens is irrigated using large, rolling pivot systems. The largest of these pivot devices can irrigate 100 acres. The farm has thirty wells, most of them about 400 feet deep, and the irrigators, when running, can distribute 1,200 gallons of water per minute. That means that in a period of 16 hours about ½ inch of water can be placed on an entire crop. These irrigators cannot make a complete circle, so about one fourth of each field is planted in pines. Terrell likes the idea that this preserves some wildlife habitat on their land. During dry periods the crops must be watered, sometimes every day. One of the advantages of this part of Georgia is the good groundwater supply. Terrell is a bit irritated by the recent government efforts to regulate water extraction, brought on by the government's concern that the local groundwater levels are sinking.

During the 60 days prior to the first harvest of leaves, farmers apply a common organic pest control called *Bacillus thuringiensis*, using a sprayer. The worst threat to collard leaves is the larvae of the diamondback moth, but the cabbage looper is also a problem. Terrell minimizes his use of conventional (organophosphate) pesticides. Instead, he introduces a biological control in the form of a small parasitic wasp called *Cotesia marginiventris*, purchased from a Texas firm called Biofac. Although they are expensive, the overall cost is reduced, since purchases of chemical pesticides are avoided. This "beneficial insect" is quite successful for the Roberson Farm, but state agents show little interest in promoting it, perhaps because they are encouraged by the large chemical suppliers to promote conventional pesticides. In addition to targeting wasps, which prey on the moths whose larvae eat his greens, Terrell also sets out special traps to capture moths. The only season when the farm faces serious insect threats is the dry late summer months. If the leaves are allowed to get particularly dry, they can become quickly infested with the diamondback worms, and the crop may be lost.

Once the leaves are large enough (about 10 inches long), hand-cutting is done by groups of "cutters." These workers use a blade to cut most of the leaves from each plant, with the exception of the top "buds," which must remain so that the plant will continue to grow more leaves.

Peak demand for collard greens occurs in late November and December, perhaps because they are believed to taste better after frosty nights, in addition to the holiday demand. The climate in southern Georgia is good for collard production because there are always some winter nights with temperatures around freezing, improving sweetness. Destructive deep freezes are quite rare. The last one, with a temperature of 4 degrees Fahrenheit, occurred in 1983.

During peak harvest periods, the company may set up powerful lights to allow picking to continue until as late as midnight. Even in dim light, harvesting is rather easy, since because only rarely do any of the collard leaves have flaws severe enough to prevent their sale. Therefore, cutters don't have to spend time selecting good leaves. Whether they are working in the day or night, cutters are motivated to work fast because they can make more money based on the amount of collards harvested, in addition to a guaranteed wage. As the leaves are cut, the cutters place them in boxes immediately. Full boxes are loaded onto a nearby truck by workers deemed too slow to harvest. The leaves are chilled as soon as possible to below 40 degrees Fahrenheit in refrigerated buildings. Otherwise, they wilt and cannot be restored to original health (see fig. 11).

Once they've been trucked back to the main farm buildings, the collards have two possible destinies: loose leaves or cleaned, chopped, and bagged leaves, generally called "ready to cook." The loose leaves are washed and packed in ice and then stored in refrigerated buildings to be kept at a constant 35 degrees Fahrenheit until being loaded onto a refrigerated tractor trailer. The "ready to cook" greens go through a large, complex machine:

Workers dump leaves from field boxes into large plastic canisters (like a colander the size of a large garbage can), which are then placed into a giant spinner (like a giant salad spinner) for washing. The leaves then move up a clean rubber conveyor to the top of the 15-foot-tall, 30-foot-long machine where they get chopped into pieces, weighed into one- or two-pound quantities, and deposited and sealed in plastic bags. The sealed bags are checked by workers for quality control and then placed in boxes with ice and stored until time for loading on a truck. Terrell sees a steady trend away from loose leaves and eventually towards precut collards.

Roberson sells to a number of wholesalers, including Green Giant and B & B Farms. The company's number one metro area for sales is Chicago, but the collards go to many cities around the country. Competition for these buyers of collards is intense, and Terrell and his brother Sid tend to focus on trends in demand, although they do no direct marketing.

W. P. RAWL & SONS, INC.—AMERICA'S BIGGEST COLLARD GROWER

In Lexington County, South Carolina, some 12 miles west of Columbia, brothers Harvey C. and Walter P. Rawl chose to build separate family farms during the 1930s. Today, they produce more collards than any other business in the country. Although they remained socially connected through regular Rawl family reunions, the two farms have grown as separate enterprises over the last 70 years. Harvey's son Clayton is now the proprietor of the Henry C. Rawl firm, and Harvey's grandsons Chris and Spanky currently run the business on several hundred acres of land. Two of Walter's sons, Wayne and Howard, are current owners of the second Rawl business, W. P. Rawl & Sons, along with three children of their late sister, Sue: Bob Wingard, Charles Wingard, and Susan Clifton. Other Rawl family members hold important positions in these companies, such as Wayne's son Ashley, Director of Marketing for W. P. Rawl & Sons.

The Rawl family has been a major supporter of vegetable research programs at Clemson University in Clemson, South Carolina, and the US

Department of Agriculture. For example, current government research on a disease called bacterial leaf spot, which is a threat to all the Brassicas and leafy greens, is underwritten largely by the Rawl family.

These are big businesses: W. P. Rawl & Sons operates on several thousand acres, growing twenty-four different crops. While they also grow large amounts of squash and green onions, their largest crop by far is collards—nearly 50 percent of the firm's business is in collards, which are produced on 2,000 acres.

Just after World War II, no one would have predicted such growth in this landscape. The Sand Hills region of South Carolina is known for its poor soils, which had never been competitive in the Cotton Kingdom or the more modern soybean boom because of the soil's lack of nutrients and its poor water-holding capacity. The Rawl family had operated a Lexington County packing company that canned peaches, okra, tomatoes, and other produce since the 1930s. The company owners, Walter P. and Josephine Rawl, found profits sinking and costs rising as the packing industry grew and changed. Producers in northern states began to exploit an advantage during the longer summer days, which allowed extended harvest hours for those canners. So when this region's farmland failed to make good money under cotton, corn, or tobacco, the Rawl family decided to shift to selling fresh produce. During the 1950s, while still canning peaches, okra, and tomatoes, the company began its ascent to leadership of the state collard industry.

In those early days, the collards were shipped from the farm as open stacks in the back of flatbed trucks. The collard plants were harvested whole (unlike today's more common method of harvesting individual leaves) and bundled for sale at the Columbia Farmers' Market. Then, in the 1950s, contracts with grocery store chains began to make up the majority of the company's business after the first irrigation systems were installed and operated by W. P. Rawl. The consolidation of fields allowed even larger irrigation systems, bringing center pivot technology (which had begun in the Western states) in the 1970s. Today, the W. P. Rawl Company has some irrigators that are 1,500 feet long. Irrigation serves to guarantee an adequate water supply to the collard plants in the sandy soils, and has become so necessary that no serious commercial collard grower in the South goes without it.

According to Howard, the eldest of the Rawl family members at age 76 as well as its reigning patriarch, the company is successful because of its quality production: "I visit other farms and I often see gaps in the collard rows. On our farm I almost never see such things." His nephew Ashley points out that quality control at a Rawl farm is superior to that on most farms.

Additional evidence for an ethic of high quality is in the loyalty of the employees. One doesn't have to be a Rawl descendant to become a family member here. One of the truck drivers, Ray Cook, began driving for W. P. Rawl when he was about age 13. Today, at 47, he is still driving. Jesse, a Mexican immigrant, has worked for W. P. Rawl for 15 years, rising quickly from the rank of a farmhand to now serving as one of the farm managers, supervising a crew of twenty.

The youngest of the W. P. Rawl siblings is Joyce, born to Walter and Josephine in 1947. She is a harvest manager with a sparkle in her eye as she talks about the work. She smiles as she discusses the different ways the harvest has been done over the years. The current system is, in her opinion, a wonderful improvement over past systems. She praises the quality of the harvest crew members, nearly all of whom are originally from Mexico.

Joyce also likes the hybrid variety of collards that is now grown on the farm. "When I was younger we grew 'Champion' collards, an open-polli-nated variety. Its habit is to spread its leaves fairly widely. That means that when we harvest the plant we have to carefully fold the leaves upward, which may cause damage and also slows us down. When we switched to 'Top Bunch' in the late 1980s, we found its habit to be far more upright. During the transition when we grew both varieties, my crews and I would be so excited at the prospect of harvesting a Top Bunch field, we would cheer." Today, ninety-five percent of the W. P. Rawl crop is Top Bunch. About five percent is the Blue Max variety of collard.

There was a time when each farm tried to develop its own variety (using

Champion or some other variety as a starter) to gain an advantage over the competition. One of the main goals was to find a variety which would be slow to go to seed in spring. When a collard plant begins to flower (bolt) it no longer produces harvestable leaves. Howard has admitted that he once was caught sneaking about at night and taking a few of another farmer's best plants to try and develop a superior hybrid. He says the farmer made him throw the plants back into the field.

Some collards are planted by direct seeding, but just as often the collards are started in seed beds and then transplanted to the larger fields. If raised in seed beds, seedlings normally require about four to eight weeks before being transplanted. In the process, four- and six-row "sled transplanters" are pulled by tractors through the fields, followed by two walking crew members to correct occasional mistakes. Four to six workers will sit on the transplanter, planting a seedling every few seconds as the machine pushes dirt over the roots. This partnership of human and machine can plant six to eight acres per day.

The peak harvest season is the last two weeks of December, when collard demand in the grocery stores is at its highest. Prices are actually lowest then, but the volume sold makes up for the low price. The W. P. Rawl Company sells about 20 percent of its entire annual volume during those two weeks. Howard says that during that seasonal peak, the fields are lit up by light towers to allow night harvest by the crews. "We have to harvest only really good quality fields when we operate at night, however," said Howard. "That's because the person harvesting cannot see well enough to easily skip over stunted, diseased or damaged leaves."

The harvest is labor intensive. Field crews walk along the rows gathering leaves from the plants. They work by stripping the leaves, moving both hands with a downward motion along the stalk, but leaving both the heart and four or five other leaves at the apex so that the plant can continue to thrive. After two to six weeks, depending on the weather and the demand, the crew can return to the same plant and harvest again.

Once gathered, the leaves are grouped into sets weighing about three and a half pounds, then packed into 25-pound boxes (cardboard or plastic), and stacked on twenty-foot trailers situated in the field. These trailers are specially designed to allow efficient unloading at the farm's packing plant. Each of the trailers can hold 500 cardboard boxes. The collard leaves are then moved to the packing plant where they are refrigerated within a couple of hours of harvest—freshness is essential in this business. Some collards are washed, cut, and packed into boxes with ice, but more and more of the collards are washed, cut, bagged, and then placed in boxes. Increasing production of these "value-added" collards are a central objective for the Rawl operations because of increased interest from "convenience" shoppers—people who would normally skip collards because they don't have time to clean and cut them.

One of the secrets to success for the Rawl operations has been the shift from purely chemical pest control to "integrated pest management." Howard is proud of this shift in the approach at W. P. Rawl. "I began investigating ways to protect beneficial insects twenty years ago," he said. On the other hand, Powell Smith noted that some farmers depend so much on chemical sprays to control caterpillars that the local caterpillar population develops resistance to the chemicals and the crop can become almost impossible to protect.

Ashley Rawl told us that collards account for 40 to 50 percent of their sales. "Most of our collard business—90 percent—is to supermarkets. Our distribution is the Eastern United States, including perhaps every major grocery store chain (even Walmart). The fresh greens market is strongest in the Southeast, plus northern cities." Asked if collards are currently selling well, his response was enthusiastic. "Yes, there is quite an increased demand for collards, perhaps partly due to our new ways of marketing them (cut, cleaned, and bagged). Our company faces a challenge with prices. Input costs related to petroleum (fertilizer, transport, even rubber bands) are all much higher, so prices need to go up. And we're diversifying. This year we are growing twenty-four different items, both bulk and value added (which means cut, cleaned, bagged)."

When asked whether recent *E. coli* bacteria scares had hurt collard sales, Rawl's response was cautious: "It's hard to tell what the real impact will be. The repercussions will be far-reaching: There will be serious changes in how we are regulated. California is already increasing its regulation. We'll see more regulation on how companies handle produce. You know, there are far more people who have been helped by eating fresh vegetables than have been hurt. We hate for anyone to get sick. In the past many got sick from food-borne bacteria, but no one knew how to test for it. . . . What people need to hear is that our food supply is much safer now. We check our greens in the field before we harvest, we check it in the plant after harvesting, then we check again once they're in the bags." Wayne Rawl, Ashley's father and one of the owners, chimed in, "Even bagged collards may have seen a sales reduction after the spinach scare. Some in the produce industry are going to have to pay closer attention to what they are doing—they need to do more testing. Some firms don't test for microbes as much as we do. We have a lab in-house *and* an external audit."

When asked whether bagged collards could ultimately replace traditional bunches, Ashley said, "We might see a cycle, but after the spinach story, I think we'll see people feeling more secure with bagged produce. Bunches sold 'naked' on the supermarket shelf concern me. There is a lot we farmers can do to protect the consumer, but once it's on the shelf, the public can walk by and put their hands on everything."

As might be expected, the Rawls' company places a high priority on "greens education." Donna Rawl spends 30 hours per week going to schools, television stations, fairs, and stores talking about healthy eating. "Next week she'll be in a school doing a 'Five-a-Day' program," said Ashley. "The key for our industry is increasing consumption. The new food pyramid gave leafy greens a shot in the arm. Now, it's time for the government to put their money where their mouth is [in support of good nutrition]. I was in Washington, DC, and heard Senator Harkin, of Iowa, say—I'll never forget this—'We don't have a health care system; we have a sick care system. We've got it backwards. Until we fix that, we'll always be fighting this from the back side.' Dentists have it right—they do preventive medicine, having the patient come in every six months [before problems develop too far]. Nutrition has been neglected too long." Ashley sees the bagged greens as a major step forward. "That approach helps young people try collards. It's a lot trendier in an upscale neighborhood to put a bag in your cart than to put a big old bunch of greens in there."

Some companies sell a mix of greens as a way to interest customers, but Ashley says this practice has not done much for W. P. Rawl & Sons. "We have experimented with that, especially blending mustard and turnip, but saw little result. We tried mixing cabbage and collard, but it didn't hold up well in the bag. Collards and cabbage have different respiration rates— cabbage would brown—but we are looking for a way, since those two taste good together."

We wondered whether the decline of small home gardens has helped the produce industry. Ashley concurred, "Yes, because we see that relationship on a seasonal basis; when people's garden produce is ripe, we see a decline in demand at the stores. I think growers of collards and turnips will be the last to disappear. Those people love to be out in their gardens. But young people want convenience. Our bags are going for that crowd, but we also provide the naked bunch for the older consumer. With less prep time, collards might show up on the weeknight menu at home, whereas in the past it was only on the weekend when they had time to do the washing and cutting."

In the Southeast, commercial collards are a major part of the leafy greens business, but they don't have to be grown in the main region of demand. Both Rawl and Roberson face competition, even in the South, from other wholesale companies. Firms in Texas and California now ship bagged leafy greens, including collards, to every US city. Dealing in large volumes is one strategy, but long-distance shippers also depend on the subsidies of oil, which keep fuel prices artificially low. Finally, inexpensive farm labor is found in greater supply in the Southwest. Even Mexican collards are shipped into various US supermarkets. According to Red Book Credit Services, a registration firm for buyers of wholesale produce, there were ninety-seven wholesale produce distributors in the United States who claimed to ship collards in 2012. Surprisingly, seventeen of those collard shippers—almost 20 percent—were shipping from Mexico. So Rawl and Roberson cannot presume that they will keep their strong positions in the greens market. The increasing globalization of our food commodity chains is generally accepted uncritically; those are details that few grocery store customers have cared to know. But these changes have environmental and economic costs not included in the retail price.

The imported food seems cheap because the sticker price is what most of us consider, but there are many externalities (real costs not counted in the purchase price). Imported and cross-country food shipments are contributing significantly to our country's air pollution, our problematic dependence on imported oil, high rates of illness among farmworkers where safety regulations are few or unenforced, and the continued impoverishment of our farming communities close to home. Imagine a future when all or nearly all produce might be imported from other countries. Knowing how much the world has already changed, it does seem possible that we could lose the majority of our country's commercial vegetable production, but then the costs of that kind of global food system would likely come back to haunt us: potentially, more *E. coli* outbreaks, more rural poverty, more entanglements in foreign oil political crises, and even greater alienation from the land that feeds us.

There *are* people out there—and not just parents or school nutritionists —trying to get everyone to eat more nutritious greens. They are members of the National Leafy Greens Council, founded in 1974, which is hoping to increase sales for its industry through advertising and lobbying. Most high-value commodities (e.g., cars and real estate) are promoted by individual firms or agents. But low-value vegetables are usually bought without brand identity; leafy greens such as collards are mostly bought as anonymous items on the supermarket shelf. So the National Leafy Greens Council works to get the word out for all these items. It is one force—one of the few organized ones—in the business of commercializing collards.

Rural communities have often fought off the expansion of commerce into daily life. Historian Jack Kirby quotes a North Carolina sharecropper in 1938 as saying, "We country folks ain't like you town folks. We don't have to run to the store every time we get hungry. We go to our smokehouse for meat, to the henhouse for chicken and eggs, to the cows for milk an' butter; send our own wheat an' corn to the mill for flour an' meal; have gardens an' orchards for vegetables, fruit; in winter there's canned stuff, potatoes, plenty of cabbage, collards, turnips, an' our firewood grows all 'round us. I don't see how you town folks live when you have to spend money for everything, even dried beans an' peas."[5]

Collards actually had a business angle in the rural South long before this man's claim was recorded. Rural families have long traditions in both commercial and self-sufficient farming; therefore, many collard gardens have served both purposes. Selling some of your family garden produce is often considered an honorable form of ambition, and conversely, a market gardener is not ostracized for eating part of his commercial harvest.

But commercialization of the collard came later for many other southern vegetables. In northern cities there was little—or no—demand, and even in southern cities the commercial demand only rose appreciably after the 1880s. One reason may be that leafy greens such as collards are more fragile than most produce. Certainly retailers who tried would have discovered that other vegetables, such as cabbages, sweet corn, and beans, were far easier to store and transport.

Even today few investors are interested in the risky world of vegetable farming. The return from most farm products is so low that only large, highly capitalized farms can survive. This means such relatively low-value vegetables as collards are very challenging as a business venture. The profit margins are very small, and, of course, the risk of a failed crop is very high. Consequently, we are not surprised to find only a few large growers attempting to supply distant markets with fresh collards.

Consider the grower's share of the sale price: for collards, this is about 26 cents on the dollar; by contrast, the grower's share for onions is 32 cents.[6] As every farmer knows, the up-front investment in a crop is always required, but the sale is never guaranteed, so minimizing risk is a constant goal. Since World War II, many small farms have been sold, often to owners of larger farms. In order to reduce risk of a bad sale, agribusinesses seek crop mixes that can be altered each year to match shifting prices. Commercial collards have often become just one more crop on very large diversified farms that grow a dozen different vegetables, varying their mix every year.

The growth of supermarkets is central to the modern American food chain. It has been said that without them, most modern Americans would simply starve.[7] In fact, a lover of collards can move just about anywhere in the South and not starve—or even suffer from hunger. Our research has found that supermarket collards are ubiquitous, with sample data suggesting that nearly every corner of the South has a supermarket selling collards in the fresh produce, freezer, and/or canned goods section. In the large cities outside the South, collards have become standard in produce sections, mainly to satisfy customers who moved there from the South—but also, we suspect, to demonstrate to customers that the store has every kind of produce you could ever desire.

Collards Shipped from Georgia to Chicago

Every December, the *Chicago Sun-Times* often includes a full-page advertisement for a small chain of meat and grocery stores named Moo & Oink. The chain has three stores in Chicago—two on the Southside and one on the Westside—and they market themselves to the large African American customer base of the city. The advertisement includes, among many other items, pigs' feet, pigs' ears, chitterlings, sweet potatoes, and collard greens. Their price for collard greens in 2009 was 39 cents per pound, which was the lowest of anywhere in the country. This is what the food industry calls a "loss leader"—a product priced low to get customers into a store so they will buy other items, including more profitable ones. A visit to the Westside store on a Saturday in late December finds the place bustling with customers.

Kevin Williams, the produce manager for all three stores, who has worked for Moo & Oink for seventeen years, is right inside the entrance at the produce section, tending to his displays. "This store is only six years old, but it leads the other two locations in produce sales," Williams told us, "and collard greens are one of the most popular items. I sell at least two hundred cases a week [at twenty-five pounds a case] throughout the year, and far more than that during the peak times. This Thanksgiving, we couldn't keep the collards coming out fast enough. We couldn't even get through the crowd to put them into the showcase." Thanksgiving is the highest peak time for collard sales at Moo & Oink, when weekly sales have reached as much as 650 cases. The Christmas and New Year's peaks are much lower, with about 300 to 350 cases each. Why might collards be more popular than turnip and mustard greens? Williams answered, "They're easier to clean. All the soul food restaurants around here offer collards, and I figure that's why. And I think collards just taste better. To me, the kale, cabbage, or spinach will smell bad when you cook them" (see fig. 15).

Other greens sell well here, too, including turnip greens and mustard greens (a hundred cases a week for each) and, to a lesser extent, kale and slick-leaf mustard greens. Indeed, at the two Southside locations, Williams finds collards sales are lower, about even with turnip or mustard greens. He wonders out loud why the Westside location had such high collard sales. His theory is that the Westside residents migrated more recently from the South and that the Southside residents are two or three generations removed from their Southern roots.

Moo & Oink gives clear priority to meat sales but also sells a great deal of produce. There is a connection, said Williams: "People use our smoked meats to cook their collards. We have about $20,000 in produce sales from this store every week."

The main supplier for all these greens is Roberson Farms. Williams said, "We buy our collards normally at 29 cents a pound. That can go up when there is a freeze in Georgia. Sometimes we just can't get collards from Georgia. In January and February of last year, we could get none from Georgia and ended up buying all our collards from Texas at a higher price."

Restaurant Collards

The shift to eating in restaurants has changed many aspects of Southern culture—fewer home-cooked meals means lower collard consumption, since most chain restaurants do not offer collards. But the down-home or "meat-and-three" restaurants are still out there, and many sell cooked greens (see map 1).

In an effort to increase our understanding of greens in the South, from 2006 to 2008 we surveyed by phone several hundred restaurants around the South, asking the cook, owner or manager what greens they served. Hoping to discover which greens are in demand by locals, we surveyed only "down-home" or "country" restaurants and avoided chains. We sought a broad, complete survey of such restaurants in nearly every county of 10 Southern states, sampling no fewer than two or three per county. In Mississippi, excellent geographic coverage gave a reliable picture of consumption.

Our questions were simple: Do you serve greens? If so, what kind(s)? Is that daily, or particular days of the week? Can you tell us what kind of restaurant you have? We allowed the restaurant employee or owner on the phone to assume we were a potential customer. We collected data on 90 down-home restaurants across the state of Mississippi by visiting or calling and speaking with the cook, manager, or owner.

At the Country Platter in Cleveland, Mississippi, turnip or mustard greens are on the buffet on Mondays and Tuesdays. It's the same at Christine's Back Porch in Canton. At Mr. D's Old Country Store in Port Gibson, there are only mustard greens on the buffet, but they're available every day. Little Wimp's Bar-B-Q House in Belzoni offers more variety: they rotate between the three greens (turnip, mustard, and collard). The cook at Jeem's Diner in Greenwood likes to offer a mix of turnip and mustard greens but prepares collard greens only for Fridays. The Blue & White in Tunica keeps it simple: only turnip greens, every day of the week. A breakdown of the Mississippi down-home restaurants by type of greens served shows that of the 90 restaurants surveyed, just over half serve only turnip greens. That result indicates that Mississippi is mainly a turnip greens state.

But people also like variety—or restaurants are hedging their bets—
because a quarter of the local restaurants offer all three greens. Just a tenth
of the restaurants surveyed offer turnip and mustard greens, but not collards. The surprising result was that not one of the ninety restaurants surveyed in Mississippi offered *only* collards. We had to continue searching for
the true heart of collard country.

Down-home Restaurants as a Measure of People's Preferences

Our survey began with the assumption that these local restaurants are serving what local people prefer, but we also knew from driving all around Mississippi that turnips are far more popular than collards among those who
raise a garden. In fact, this survey of down-home restaurants confirms that
Mississippi and Tennessee are both more turnip green states. For Georgia,
we were able to survey a total of one hundred and thirty-nine restaurants, at
least one in most of the state's one hundred and fifty-nine counties, although
some counties did not seem to have a true down-home restaurant (see table
9). This data suggests that both turnips and collards are popular in Georgia. In fact, 77 percent of our surveyed down-home restaurants in that state
offer either turnip greens, collard greens, or both. Another way of considering the data is that 71 percent of the restaurants offered turnips, while only
63 percent offered collards. Mustard greens, always coming in third place at
the state level, were available at only 17 of the down-home restaurants—and
mostly where the other greens were also offered. Those Georgia restaurants
that did not offer greens were often those serving a limited menu, featuring
barbeque or simple grilled items such as hamburgers.

We should not assume too much about the choices made by cooks in
these down-home restaurants, as they may not be local folk or may not care
to reflect the local food preferences on their menu. But we have been able to
consider a wide range of cultural indicators. So our collard map, taken with
a grain of salt and a touch of pepper, suggests where the true core of collard
culture can be found.

TABLE 9. PROFILE OF GREENS SERVED IN "DOWN-HOME" RESTAURANTS IN GEORGIA*

Type of Greens	# of Restaurants	% of All Restaurants
Collards & Turnips	44	32
Turnips Only	36	26
Collards Only	26	19
Collards, Turnips, & Mustard	12	9
Mustard & Turnips	5	4
Collards & Mustard	4	3
Mustard Only	2	1
No Greens Served	10	7

*From our survey of at least one in 136 of the state's 159 counties

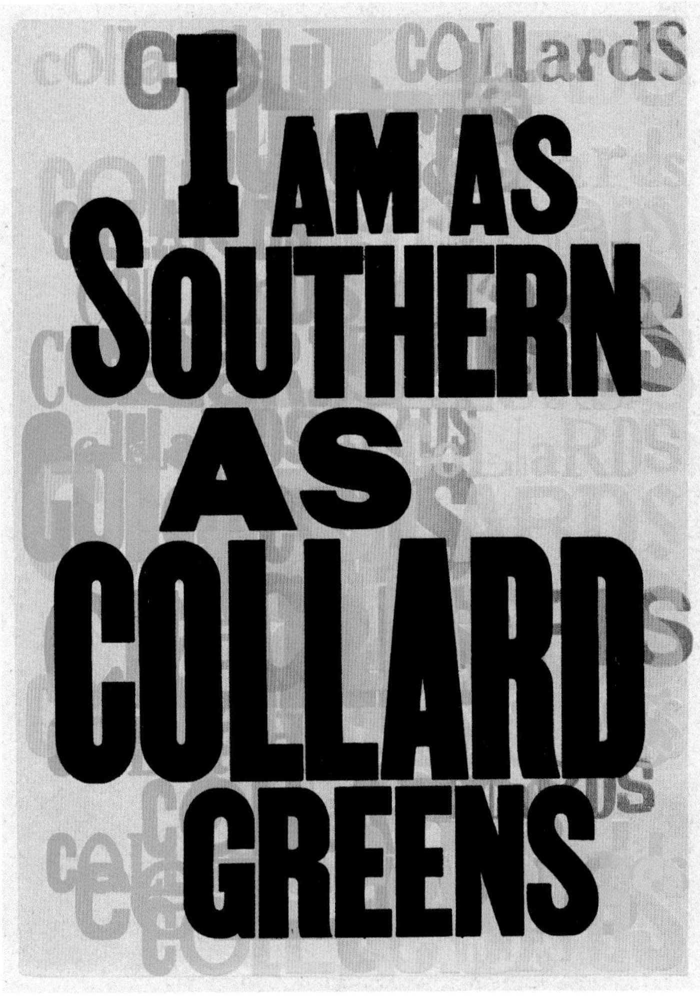

FIG. 1. Letterpress print by Amos Paul Kennedy Jr.

FIG. 2. Collard Festival parade float with royalty, Ayden, North Carolina.

Photo courtesy of Edward H. Davis

FIG. 3. Cecil Stroud in his collard patch in Duplin County, Eastern North Carolina.

Photo courtesy of John T. Morgan

FIG. 4. Annie Morgan demonstrates four stages in a traditional cooking method for collard greens.

a: Pick, clean, and sort collard leaves fresh from the garden.

b & c: Bring collards to a boil in a large pot with salted water. Cover, cook until tender, and add flavorings.

d: Using two knives, cut greens into bite-sized pieces.

Photos courtesy of John T. Morgan

Top: FIG. 5. Bum Dennis in his restaurant kitchen
with a pan of hot collards, Ayden, North Carolina.

Bottom: FIG. 6. Ella Woods of Evergreen, Alabama, with her ornamental collard plants.

Photos courtesy of Edward H. Davis

FIG. 7. Leading leafy greens. *From left:* spinach, kale, collard, mustard, and turnip.

Photo courtesy of Samuel B. Davis

FIG. 8. Bulk collard seeds for sale in a rural hardware store.

Photo courtesy of Edward H. Davis

Left: FIG. 9. Helen Mason and Agricultural Extension Agent Bobby Wilson in a community garden for Atlanta's public housing. Wilson has helped establish over two hundred such gardens.

Right: FIG. 10. In Mound Bayou, Mississippi, a single row of healthy collards tended by Mattie Brown.

Photos courtesy of Edward H. Davis

FIG. 11. Crates of collards just harvested; Wendell Roberson Farms, Tifton, Georgia.

Photo courtesy of Edward H. Davis

FIG. 12. Fresh collards and precut and packaged collards for sale at a
Piggly Wiggly grocery store in Tuscaloosa, Alabama.

Photo courtesy of Allie L. Harper

FIG. 13. Collard bunches for sale in January at the Riverwalk
Farmers' Market in Tuscaloosa, Alabama.

Photo courtesy of Allie L. Harper

FIG. 14. Roberson commercial collard crop with four weeks of growth in Tifton, Georgia.
Photo courtesy of Edward H. Davis

FIG. 15. Kevin Williams, Chicago produce manager, with Roberson collards from Georgia.

Photo courtesy of Edward H. Davis

Above: FIG. 16. Seed-saver Bud Dew, outside Tarboro, North Carolina, tills his field but leaves the best row of collards to allow them to generate new seeds. This row will produce many thousands of seeds, so he only has to do this every few years.

Photo courtesy of John T. Morgan

Opposite: FIG. 17. An experimental plot with over 60 different heirloom collards collected from gardeners around the South by the authors and their colleagues. This plot is in Charleston, South Carolina, and run by Dr. Mark Farnham of the USDA. The short row in the foreground is from seed-saver Gerald Brown.

Photo courtesy of Edward H. Davis

FIG. 18. J. D. Futrell, a seed saver, with his "henpecked" (spotted) collards, Richlands, North Carolina.

Photo courtesy of John T. Morgan

FIG. 19. Charlie Malone of Northport, Alabama, with his purple collards.

Photo courtesy of Edward H. Davis

Top: FIG. 20. Some consumers prefer the yellow cabbage collard for its milder flavor.

Bottom: FIG. 21. Leaves of six different collard landraces collected from seed savers in Mississippi, Alabama, South Carolina, and North Carolina.

Photos courtesy of Edward H. Davis

Top: FIG. 22. Ancestor of the collard, the colewort, in a 1380s woodprint in the *Tacuinum Sanitatis*, Lombardy, Italy. Image courtesy of Bibliothèque nationale de France, Paris

Bottom: FIG. 23. Gardener near Lisbon, Portugal, with heirloom collards.

Photo courtesy of Edward H. Davis

Top: FIG. 24. Freshly picked collards for sale at the
Carrboro, North Carolina, Farmers' Market.
Photo courtesy of Bradley A. Crittenden

Bottom: FIG. 25. Collards sold on the honor system near Havana
on the Florida Panhandle. Photo courtesy of Chris and Steve Lindeman

FIG. 26. Reanell Bradley of Wisacky, South Carolina, with her collards.

Photo courtesy of John T. Morgan

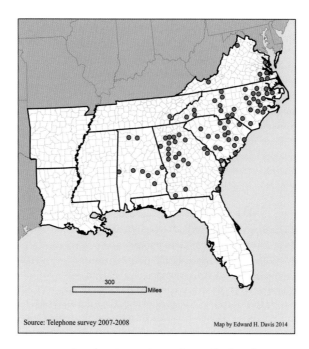

MAP I. Local restaurants serving collards, where
collards are the main or only cooked greens

All maps courtesy of Edward H. Davis

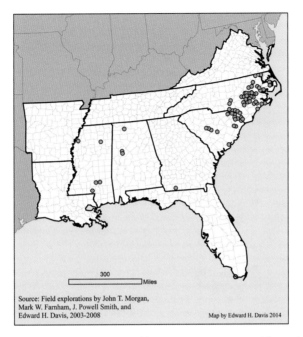

MAP 2. Collard seed savers discovered by Morgan, Davis, Smith, and Farnham

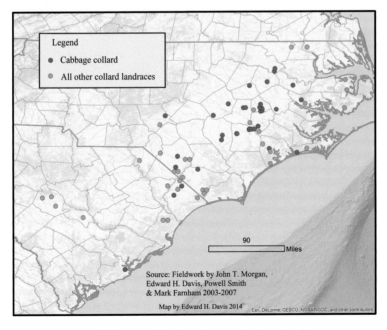

MAP 3. Cabbage collard seed savers in the Carolinas

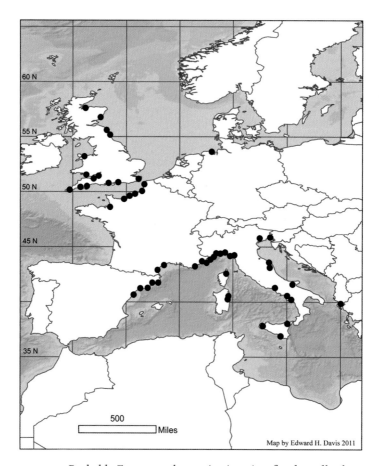

MAP 4. Probable European domestication sites for the collards

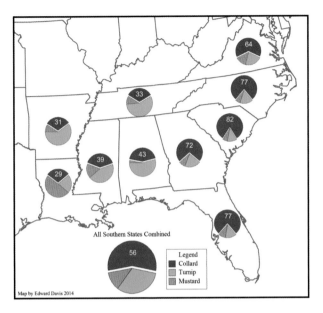

MAP 5. College students' preferences for greens, by state

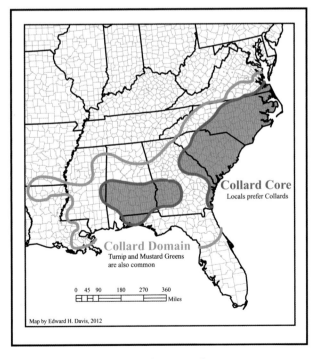

MAP 6. Collard Core and Domain

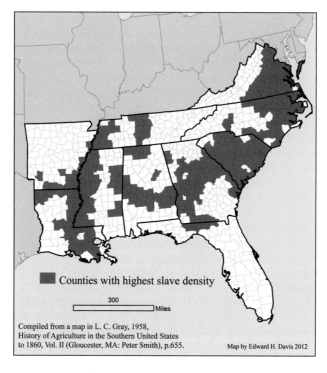

Counties with highest slave density

300
Miles

Compiled from a map in L. C. Gray, 1958,
History of Agriculture in the Southern United States
to 1860, Vol. II (Gloucester, MA: Peter Smith), p.655.   Map by Edward H. Davis 2012

MAP 7. Slave population concentrations in 1860

6

Saving Collard Seed

The Essential Act in Food Heritage

THE BUSINESS OF COLLARD SEED

Cairo (pronounced kay'row) in southwestern Georgia was once the "World's Collard Seed Center."[1] If one bought collard seed in America anytime between the 1880s and the 1950s, it was likely a variety called "Georgia collard" that came from Cairo. In fact, Georgia collard farmers sold seed to national seed companies as far back as the 1840s.[2] Sales of collard seed increased significantly after the Civil War, and one study of southern country stores at the close of the 19th century found that collard seeds were among the prominent items regularly sold.[3]

Throughout the first decades in America's history, most gardeners saved their own seed or got a supply from a seed-saving friend. When industrialization picked up in the 1870s and especially after World War I, the urban demand for fresh produce was booming; refugees from rural America craved their traditional fresh garden vegetables. Urban grocery stores and town markets could sell collards, and commercial growers, such as gardeners, began to buy larger quantities of seed. Because southern Georgia has a long growing season, hundreds of acres of collards were being grown on the many small farms of Grady County and the neighboring region.

Recognizing a unique opportunity, some enterprising wholesalers—businessmen with local contacts, warehouses, and equipment—contracted with local farmers for their seed, offering them a chance to earn money twice in a year from the same field. Here's how a double-purpose field could work: the farmer would plant up to five acres of greens in summer and then harvest the leaves for shipping to urban markets in November through March. Unlike heading cabbage, collards can be harvested of their leaves multiple times, allowing for a constant crop of greens over a period of months, if the weather cooperates. Such a characteristic always appeals to thrifty gardeners; some varieties of collards in England were even sold under the name "cut-and-come-again." In early twentieth-century Georgia, this process made good business sense: if a farmer left the plants in the field after the last March harvest, they would flower in the spring and be ready for a seed harvest by August—a second income from the same field in a tidy twelve-month cycle.

In Cairo, Howard Thrower witnessed the final decades of the collard seed business. He had worked from 1946 to 1965 as the warehouse manager for W. H. Robinson, a merchant who also had a large pecan wholesale and shipping firm.

Because the early Southern collard seed industry was conducted by handshake agreements between hundreds of farmers and about half a dozen wholesalers (W. H. Robinson and Richter Brothers were the major firms), a wholesaler could come directly to a farm with a tractor-pulled combine fitted with wooden paddles. The paddles would thrash the dry seed-pods, and seeds would drop into burlap bags fitted onto the combine. A normal crop of seed was 700 pounds per acre, but some farms produced 1,000 pounds per acre. The volume is impressive when you consider that each pound is between 112,000 and 120,000 seeds. So one acre of collards could potentially yield 120 million seeds. Also impressive is the return on the original seed: a farmer need only plant one to three pounds of seed to produce each acre of collards.

During the 1930s and 1940s, a farmer was usually getting 10 cents a pound, which would bring only $100 gross per acre—not a get-rich scheme by any means, but at least a second income from one field. At the warehouse, the wholesale companies used hand-cranked (later electric) cleaning machines to separate the seed from the chaff. These cleaners produced seed of various grades, which brought prices from the seed retailers of about 20 cents a pound. Vegetable seed sells cheaply because large volumes can be produced easily, and a bad year or two can lead to a crisis of sorts.

During World War II, several wholesalers ran advertisements in the Cairo newspaper saying that there was a collard and collard seed shortage. This alarming ad by the Richter Bros. firm in Cairo appeared October 1, 1942:

> Attention Farmers: Plant Collards! For Eating Purposes—For the
> Seed Market. Today there exists a serious shortage of Collard Seed,
> owing to the fact that for the past two years, prices of vegetables
> have been high and large numbers of farmers sold their collards for
> eating purposes, instead of for seed. Today the collard seed supply
> is practically exhausted. . . . we are paying 40 cents per pound . . .
> and unable to obtain anything like enough at that price to satisfy
> the demand. Plant collards for seed purposes . . . Higher prices
> anticipated . . .

The price given here is much higher than normal for the time, although this advertisement may not be altogether trustworthy. What is clear is the importance of the collard seed business in Cairo in those years. In fact, the record sales for W. H. Robinson would come in 1959, when the company sold 300,000 pounds to commercial seed companies, including Burpee, Hastings, and Woodruff.

Still, the informal handshake system was not creating the seed needed by modernizing agribusiness. First, mechanical seed planting devices were now commonly used on commercial farms, which meant those growers required seed of a uniform size. But Cairo wholesalers had no equipment for sorting their seed by size, as such machines were costly.

Second, although five varieties of open-pollinated seed were harvested and sold by W. H. Robinson (Georgia, Bluestem, Cabbage Collard, Louisiana Sweet, and Vates), the seed coming off the farms in each burlap bag was not pure. Thrower noticed that farmers were not careful about keeping distinct varieties at a distance from one another, so bees could visit more than one kind of collard. This meant that cross-fertilization was bound to be common, and seed sold as one type often exhibited characteristics of another. Some unreliable seed was being sold because of a lack of quality control.

Retail was also changing the seed situation after World War II. Seed retailers, including Park and Burpee, began to demand certified seed in the early 1950s; that is, seed produced under controlled and documented conditions. One of those conditions stated that no other Brassica crop could be flowering within a half-mile of the seed crop. Thrower developed a plan for this isolation, but found it difficult to force local farmers to follow suit. When he asked one woman to pull up some cabbage she had planted near her seed collards, she snapped back, "You big people think you can run over us." He later replanted her garden to make it up to her, but the picture was clear to Thrower: certified seed was beyond the capacity of the Cairo collard growers.

By the 1960s, wholesale seed businesses out West were producing certified seed of seventy types of vegetable. The seed was sorted by size on modern equipment, and although the Georgia seed was still #1, some new, more prolific hybrids (Champion and Blue Max) were accelerating on the market. The old way of doing seed business on the scale of the small local farm could no longer pass muster.

The final blow came in 1965. Robinson, who had once been called the Collard Seed King, saw his business's warehouse burned to the ground. As a result, Thrower, who had handled hundreds of tons of collard seed per year in Cairo, was sent looking for another job and became superintendent at the local country club. Today, there are no longer any significant commercial collard seed producers in Georgia or, indeed, elsewhere in the South.

The nation's "seedbed" is now Washington State, where climate conditions are optimal (mild and dry) and several large companies have mechanized their seed farms. Washington's small-seeded vegetable seed production takes place on a total of approximately 15,000 acres. Roughly thirty seed crops are produced in two primary seed-growing regions. In western Washington, growers produce seed crops on 6,000 acres spread throughout the Skagit Valley and in Lewis, Island, Snohomish, and Whatcom counties. In eastern Washington, crops are grown in the greater Columbia Basin on approximately 9,000 acres.[4]

Seed commerce is dominated today by transnational corporations with ownership of many farm inputs, from fertilizer to pesticide to seed. Consolidation and buyout in the seed industry occurred in a flurry after a 1980 Supreme Court ruling that a private company could own the genetics of a plant. Patenting the genetic code allows companies to earn more profits than ever in the seed industry because once you own such a patent, no one—farmer, breeder, gardener—can legally duplicate your plant. "Seed saving" is, in fact, outlawed, except for those few varieties not under patent. Today, only about ten companies still produce collard seed commercially in the United States, and Seminis, the world's largest seed company, controls about 40 percent of the US seed market. The name Seminis will not easily be found on a retail seed packet, since numerous subsidiaries wholly owned by Seminis continue to operate under their own names. In fact, Seminis is actually, in turn, a subsidiary of Monsanto.[5]

It does, indeed, seem ironic that seed for a plant so identified with the South comes from the Pacific Northwest. One of the oldest of the region's seed companies is the Alf Christianson Seed Company of Mount Vernon, Washington. This firm was purchased by Sakata Seed Company of Japan in 2002, yet the subsidiary still sells under its original name. Their *Vegetable Seed Guide*, marketed to commercial growers (their main customers), lists the following varieties of collard green:

1. Champion, slow bolting, more uniform than Vates, winter hardy, high yield
2. Hybrid Top Bunch, matures earlier than Vates, uniform, the leading commercial

3. Hybrid Flash, uniform, slowest to bolt, allows repeated heavy harvest
4. Georgia, tolerates extreme weather, rapid growth, gardener's choice
5. Green Glaze, small bright, glossy, no bloom, garden variety
6. Morris Heading, large breed, fast growing, winter hardy
7. Vates, widely adopted, durable, heavy yield, open-pollinated
8. Blue Max, highly productive F1 hybrid (also called Hi-Crop)
9. Heavy Crop, productive, with uniform growth habit

Notice that the most common concern is uniformity, since commerce requires this characteristic above all. Apparently all varieties are considered tasty enough that distinctions of flavor are not even mentioned here. The large seed producers currently maintain three non-hybrid collards—Georgia, Green Glaze, and Vates—but these are for the less lucrative home garden market and may not be continued for long. Some traditional gardeners interviewed already prefer hybrids such as Blue Max and Top Bunch because they can grow larger than open-pollinated varieties.[6]

Commercial seed production is now uprooted from the South, its cultural hearth, because the possibility of a good financial return is low. Since all vegetable seed is trending towards globalization, perhaps collard seed will once again be a foreign import, as it was in the colonial era. Because collard seed is now patented and sold by global business rather than simply raised and shared among friends and family, the collard may never be as southern as it was a hundred years ago.

In spite of these trends, particular kinds of collard are recognized as special by both producers and consumers, and some growers will guard their seed as they would a cherished child. Some growers want to keep their collard seed only for themselves—maybe that's to keep it out of the hands of the competition. Or perhaps it is a sense that their collard is a true heirloom—a keepsake from their ancestors (see fig. 16).

In the hamlet of Alligator, in cotton-growing Bolivar County, Mississippi, just east of the Mississippi River, Thomas Heags, who tends a kitchen garden and lives alone in a tiny house at the end of a sandy lane, has saved seed of various vegetables all his life. He recalls buying his collard seed from a seed saver around 1955, and he has saved seed from that collard approximately once every five years since then. Each year, he grows a row of twenty-five or so collard plants, in addition to a patch of mustard and turnips.

Heags is typical of the many seed savers we interviewed. He is passionate about getting fresh produce from his own garden for his home-cooked meals. He is independent in his lifestyle, avoiding the modern habit of buying unessential commodities. We interviewed more than eighty seed savers, many of whom shared collard seeds with us. Astonishing as it may seem, the quiet work of Heags and other seed savers like him may one day salvage farm crops from disease and pest problems in countries around the globe.

Elbin McLaurin, an elderly man who lives in tiny Soso, Mississippi, epitomizes the value of seed savers to our culture. He keeps a garden as his favorite hobby, a plot 35 feet by 100 feet, with rows of collards, cabbages, and mustard greens. The collards were obviously not a standard hybrid cultivar purchased from a retailer because they exhibited color and size variations in the rows, a sure sign of rich genetic diversity indicating a local "heirloom" landrace. A landrace is a population of a cultivated plant or animal that has adapted in one area over a long period without formal breeding methods. Geneticists have been studying landraces for many decades as resources for breeding to improve disease and pest resistance in crops.

In gathering saved seeds, Elbin chooses particular collard plants to flower and then form seed heads. This decision is generally made in March when the garden is being prepared for spring crops. Maintaining a group of aging collard plants at this time can be a burden, since good garden soil and space may be scarce; but for some gardeners, if the weather has cooperated, even in March there will be collard leaves to harvest. Elbin is ambitious in his seed saving, setting aside sixty plants. Professional breeders raise a minimum of 150 plants for a single variety.

The plants Elbin selects for flowering are those he believes are healthiest at the time. He looks for leaves that are bright green, lacking in blemish, firm, and "a little spongy to the touch." These plants have the traits he wants to maintain in his collards. As the early summer arrives, a five-foot stalk has become established and upon it are large numbers of small yellow flowers, each with four petals. These are, with any luck, visited by many bees, which pollinate the plants, distributing genetic information among the full set of collard plants. Once fertilized, the flower stalk produces a number of pods, or siliques, that contain the seeds. By midsummer, these pods dry out and open up, releasing the seeds. A seed saver must be ready to collect the seed before it is lost on the ground.

At age 76, Elbin says he won't likely pass his hobby down to anyone else because his daughters and friends are not interested. But he loves to relate how he got his seed in the first place. "Miss Tabitha (pronounced 'tuh-bye-tha') Dykes was a wonderful soul who shared her collard seed with people all around here. I reckon many people she knew never had to buy seed at all. She was the most generous person I have known. Maybe that's why she lived so long: she was born in 1886 and died in 1986. So far as I know, her collard goes back to her childhood in the 1800s. She must have gotten it from her mama."

When we asked Elbin for a sample of his seed, he asked me how much we would like. We suggested a tablespoon. As generous as his late friend Tabitha, Elbin insisted on giving me a bag of seed weighing over a pound, which contains more than 100,000 seeds.

The Collard Seed Savers Project

Certainly seed saving is one of the oldest traditions in the South. It is done by less than one percent of gardeners—and even among seed savers, collard seed saving is rare, for it requires a fair amount of effort and results in only insignificant monetary savings. But there are other benefits, as to which the examples above testify: the gardener enjoys a favorite flavor, has a reliable plant well-adapted to local soil and climate, and may have fewer pest problems since the plant will be hardier.

From 2003 to 2007 we conducted field research, along with Dr. Mark Farnham of the US Department of Agriculture (USDA), to search out and locate collard seed savers in the Southeast. The work was supported by a grant from the USDA Economic Research Service, which is preserving heirloom varieties in the USDA's seed storage facility (namely the National Center for Genetic Resources Preservation) in Geneva, New York. The center's purpose is preservation of a bank of biodiversity that may be drawn upon in the future to develop disease-resistant and pest-resistant varieties of plants (see fig. 17).

The plants grown on farms and in gardens around the world are becoming overall less diverse because small numbers of commercial hybrid varieties for each crop plant are becoming increasingly more adopted.[7] This homogenizing trend is true for collards. Seed companies offer fewer varieties, and seed saving is a dying tradition. With only a handful of varieties being grown by most commercial growers, we now have a collard crop that is quite vulnerable to major disease or pest threats. Lack of crop diversity means easy predation by any well-adapted new pest or disease.

Figure 21 depicts six of the ninety different landraces grown by Dr. Mark Farnham at the USDA Vegetable Laboratory in Charleston, South Carolina, from seed collected by the authors from southeastern seed savers. The wide variation among heirloom collard leaves comes as a surprise even to experienced gardeners.

In searching for fall and winter collard gardens that expressed the characteristics of heirloom collards—great variability in size and color—we found ninety-seven seed savers, mostly in the Carolinas where we had begun our work and advertised our search in local newspapers. There were also seed savers in Mississippi (six), Alabama (eight), and Georgia (three). We found not only a great diversity of seed, but also considerable diversity among the seed savers: men and women, black and white. If our findings are at all representative, one characteristic describes all seed savers: they are, simply put, old, with an average age of 70. One example is J. D. Futrell of Richlands, North Carolina (see fig. 18). He is rightly proud of his "henpecked" collard,

so called because of the spots on the leaves. At over 75, Futrell cannot, if he
works alone, keep his heirloom collards viable much longer.

It is possible that a significant number of young seed savers simply
evaded our detection. There are reports of a small subculture of seed savers that includes young urban people interested in organic and sustainable
methods; however, our searching turned up only a few seed savers from this
younger demographic.[8] A geographic bias is also likely due to our greater
outreach in the Carolinas. Our windshield survey of the Deep South states
was much less fruitful, and even multiple inquiries to gardening scholars
turned up few collard seed savers. The results of our search for collard seed
savers are analyzed in map 2.

Why would the Carolinas' coastal plain have more collard seed savers
than other Southern states? Perhaps the timing of settlement is relevant.
Since commercial seed became more widely available after the Civil War,
part of the Deep South, without stable settlement before 1860, might not
have had enough time for the development of a gardening and seed-saving
custom. Secondly, in parts of the South, the density of small farms is low
and has been such since well before the Civil War. In some cases this was
because of the large size of plantations, and in other cases it was due to poor
soils, large cattle ranches, or commercial timber. These phenomena would
limit our chances of discovering seed savers in those areas. And finally, seed
saving might have been discouraged by slave owners, as they sought to deny
slaves the resources of independence. Surely many slaves and poor whites
saved seed anyway, but their free time was so limited that many must have
been unable to garden, and when the war ended and freedom came, those
who became tenant farmers were often unskilled at gardening and would
have had little access to seeds worth saving. A survey of black tenant farms
in central Alabama by the Tuskegee Institute in 1898 found that most did
not have a garden.[9] Extreme poverty and lack of education may have broken
most garden traditions in these former slave households. These conditions
could have applied also to poor white rural families.

Seed savers appear to have been much more common in parts of the

Carolina coastal plains. These areas have a high density of small farms, both yeoman and small-holder, and were settled during the colonial era, so they had more time to develop gardens. Based on the seed saver interviews conducted, we also believe there is a long history there of informal networks among gardeners who shared seeds.

Mark Farnham is excited about the potential of the collected seeds: "Based on the diverse appearances that we have observed among these collard landraces, one has to assume there is significant genetic diversity for the traits exhibited, as well as for the traits not seen, like disease resistance or nutritional quality." It is too early in the testing to know about these characteristics, according to Farnham. "Resistance to a disease like black rot could be important for collard improvement, but it could just as easily be important for broccoli, cabbage, and cauliflower since collard is easily crossed with these other types of the species. The broccoli and cabbage family represents a billion dollar vegetable industry in the United States, so it's easy to see the potential impact."[10]

Most landraces of collard are so particular to a place and a small network of people in that place that they acquire unique names by which the growers identify them. Here are some examples of landraces and the people who shared them:

Big Daddy Greasy Green: Hansel Sellars, Cairo, Georgia
Bill's Pea Ridge Collard: Buddy Brickhouse, Gum Neck, North Carolina
Crinkle Leaf Collard: Alma Huffman, Richlands, North Carolina
Dark Collard: Alice and Harrell Felton, Eure, North Carolina
Georgia White Collard: Joe Long, Nakina, North Carolina
Hard Headed Cabbage Collard: Ronald Spain, Jacksonville, North Carolina
Heading (or Porth) Collard: Henry J. Sease, Gilbert, South Carolina
Nancy Wheat's Purple Collard: Mac Walter, Coker, Alabama
Old Mountain Collard: Ethel Goude, Carver's Bay, South Carolina
Old Timey Blue Collard: A.G. Collums, Houlka, Mississippi
Yellow Cabbage Collard: Cecil Stroud, Albertson, North Carolina

The Cabbage Collard

One particular collard landrace popular in a few counties of eastern North Carolina is almost unheard of elsewhere: the cabbage collard (see fig. 20). Estimated to date back more than a century, it is a cross between a cabbage and a collard that forms a slight head and tends to have a lighter color and milder, sweeter flavor than conventional collards. Many rural and small town consumers in eastern North Carolina and northeastern South Carolina prefer to eat only this type of collard, a regional foodway not previously recognized (see map 3).

The cabbage collard may not last, however. With fewer and fewer rural residents tending a home garden and chain grocery stores offering primarily collards produced from hybrid seeds, the cabbage collard is becoming more difficult to obtain.

Several commercial growers still cater to this unique local market. One is farmer Elroy Sasser, around age 60, who owns Sasser Farm in Bladen County, North Carolina. He has 550 acres of corn, soybeans, and peanuts, and also farms about three acres of collards each year. His father grew collards for local sales and Sasser has continued the tradition. He sells cabbage collards for $1.25 a head. He even sows a large collard seedling bed each year and sells those plants to others to transplant in their gardens. He finds that people like convenience, so he does not ask customers to pick their own cabbage collards, but demand for collard quality is sufficient enough that they come to his farm to buy them. Sasser has tried "Morris Heading" collards, but he says they do not perform as well as old-fashioned cabbage collards. He uses his tobacco setter to plant collards and transplants them into the fields in the first week of September. Elroy also sells his cabbage collards to the Front Porch restaurant in Elizabethtown.

Morris Improved Heading Collard

Another kind of collard was developed in the 1920s by Elisha Morris and his son, Fairley, who desired a consistent variety. At his farm near Maxton

(Scotland County), North Carolina, Elisha's great-grandson Eric Morris explained that the family developed the "Morris Heading" collard over the years through selection of a particular strain with short stems and the ability to form a rosette that was almost a head. By the late twenties the Morris Heading variety was fully developed. After Elisha died in 1933, Fairley devoted the thirties to selling and promoting the new collard. The variety's big debut came when North Carolina State University's School of Agriculture chose to include the Morris Heading on its "recommended plant variety" list in the early 1950s. Sales of the seed expanded greatly, with seed companies purchasing seed from the Morris family for several years.

But the success was short-lived as those larger companies started producing and marketing their own Morris Heading seed. Eric's father, Lawrence Morris, "tweaked" their collard in the late 1980s to produce a plant with less of a heading habit, as some customers had complained that the Morris Heading collards they purchased developed too much of a head. That particular seed may be different from seeds collected for decades by seed savers or from those sold under the name "Morris Heading" by other seed companies.

Scouting along State Highway 43 in western Alabama, we passed through the hamlet of Samantha, about 20 miles north of Tuscaloosa, and saw a beautiful collard patch surprisingly close to the highway. The owner, Charlie Malone, was out watering his plants with his son and was happy to receive an inquiry about his garden. It often attracts attention because many of his huge collards are a deep purple. Malone has some very well-nurtured soil, resulting from years of compost and care, but that would not explain the purple color (see fig. 19).

Not only were Malone's purple collards uniquely colored, but they were very large and healthy—hallmarks of heirlooms. Although purple tinting in collard leaves had been observed at times, it was thought to be caused by a mineral deficiency. But Malone's landrace was clearly a healthy collard.

Malone said he obtained the seed two years earlier from a friend. He starts the plants in paper cups at the end of June and transplants them into the garden in late July. He fertilizes the collards using a 13-10-13 mix (these numbers refer to the percent of nitrogen, phosphorous, and potassium in a bag of fertilizer) and waters them daily in the fall with a hose, and his son, Charles, carefully removes all insects by hand (no pesticides are used). Malone clips the blossoms of some and allows these to grow over a two-year period, so they are about 4 feet tall. This clipping is uncommon, but we have seen it elsewhere in places where severe cold is rare. It is assumed that in some years Malone's garden gets a cold spell too "deep" for his collards. He generously gave us a sample of his seed and also told us where we could find the source of that seed: Mac Walter.

Almost ten miles away, also in Tuscaloosa County, we found MacArthur Walter, who told us, "I was named for the general, because I was born in 1942. My wife got these collard seeds from her mother, Nancy Wheat, who was born in 1912, and she said they had been handed down for generations." Walter does all he can to keep himself independent—living "on the cheap," working as an independent flooring contractor, and growing as much food as he can. He operates his sloping 30 x 40 ft. garden simply; the only chemicals he uses are fertilizer: Miracle-Gro and nitrate of soda. To keep the bugs off his collards, he uses "just dish detergent, which works fine." Walter weeds the garden every few days with a sharp, three-pronged rake and waters it when it's dry. "But I won't begin picking collard leaves until after two or three frosts have hit them—that's when they're best." He pulls up some plants in March and sets them out in the woods to feed the deer. "That way they eat less in my garden. And I like the deer."

Once Walter grew rutabagas, cut the greens from them, cooked them like he does his collards, and then fed them to his friends, who said, "Mac, these are some tasty collards."

"Those aren't collards!" he scoffed. "They're rutabagas! You thought I'd give you my *good* greens?" So now he sometimes grows rutabagas and eats the roots and the greens. The unique purple hue in Malone's and Walter's collards are a clear sign of their genetic diversity and could indicate invisible traits such as disease resistance.

In sharp contrast to the visits with Malone and Walter, in Pender

County in southeastern North Carolina on the morning of January 24, 2005, we found some of the most pitiful collard plants we had seen to date. The leaves were all full-sized, but they were completely limp and tinged with a deadly white. The local agricultural extension agent said the crop was lost to the cold. Frost adds to the taste of collards, but there is a limit, of course. When temperatures get below 20 degrees Fahrenheit, many collard plants begin to suffer. The plants can recover if those deep frosts are just overnight; a collard plant can go limp from a hard frost, only to lift its leaves to the sun by the next afternoon, but several days below 20 degrees Fahrenheit will damage most collard plants badly enough that they won't produce well again.

That morning in Pender County, the recorded temperature was 23 degrees Fahrenheit, which would not have killed the plants. But as the cold front passed through around dawn, the winds gusted to 20 miles per hour over a couple of hours. The plants had been "blasted" by the cold and could not recover. It was the worst collard damage in the county in twenty years.

The vulnerability of a collard plant to low or high temperatures depends on many specifics, including the type of seed. One agricultural extension agent claims she's seen collards come back after temperatures dropped below 10 degrees Fahrenheit. Steven Hopp has collards thriving in his garden through even a cold winter, with many nights around 10 degrees Fahrenheit. He lives at 2,100 feet above sea level in the mountains of southwestern Virginia, where few folks grow collards. There are probably several reasons for his success: he has a hardy heirloom ("Charlie Cannon"), and he also takes very good care of his plants, growing them in high-quality soil, keeping them properly watered and free of pests (organically), and even protecting them from the wind.

Perhaps due to all of these challenges, and because so much patience is required, collard seed savers are rare in the twenty-first century. The need for biological diversity is clear, yet we witness a widening separation of our culture from the essence of our food as plants. In the next few years, we may find that only a miniscule group of southern seed savers will remain to

fulfill the task. Collard plants will persist, preserved in three or four commercial hybrids, but unless there are reversals in current trends, our rich
collard heritage—with all those different colors, tastes, leaf forms, and adaptations to weather and pests—will be lost.

7

Imagining the Early
Southern Collard
Origin and Diffusion

Wesley Greene wears nothing but handmade clothing—even his floppy felt hat is handmade—as he stands next to his garden of collards just off Duke of Gloucester Street in Colonial Williamsburg, Virginia. Wesley is the kitchen gardener for this living museum, selecting and cultivating the appropriate food plants for an eighteenth-century town. A garden historian, he spends many rainy days in Williamsburg's Rockefeller Library, researching the historical record for evidence of colonial garden plants and cultivation methods. He is one of only a few garden historians with expert knowledge of American vegetable history, including that of the collard. At Williamsburg in the fall or winter, he may busy himself with hoeing and carrying water—caring for his collard patch in his complete colonial costume. During the cold months, he also raises winter gourds and cabbages.

"But we are doing the opposite of what colonial gardeners did," Greene says. "We are trying to preserve a moment in time, to *prevent* change in our garden plants, while the colonial gardeners were trying to improve their crops and change them rapidly. They were selecting every year for better varieties, whether larger or sweeter or more tolerant of frost or drought or summer heat. They were never standing still, and neither were their plants." In the days before hybrid seed, all garden vegetables were open-pollinated, by wind or insects that interacted with neighboring plants, producing seed of a slightly different character each year. "The collard was never just one plant form, and it changed constantly. In a sense, the historic collard was really many collards."

Greene founded the Colonial Nursery at Colonial Williamsburg in 1996, but the research he has done stretches back over thirty years. A diverse array of eighteenth-century plants is documented in his remarkable book, *Vegetable Gardening the Colonial Williamsburg Way: 18th-century Methods for Today's Organic Gardeners.*[1]

The designers of the historic area have made space for only a small garden, so Greene has just two dozen collard plants. His collards are of a type called "Green Glaze," the seed for which he bought from McCormack, one of America's leading heirloom seed sources. These are supposedly descendants of the Green Glaze variety that was available as early as 1803. Wesley says, "We really don't know anything closer to what was being grown then." In fact, other historic gardens in the South also grow the Green Glaze variety, attempting to approximate the collard of the past. The challenge is that *Brassica oleracea* is a very changeable plant, capable of altering its color and shape in only a few generations, possessing remarkable variety in form and color. Gardeners of the past two centuries directed these changes, both intentionally and accidentally, as they selected seed from preferred plants rather than from plants at random. Meanwhile, the pests and diseases and even the climate and soil that helped make the plant what it is have all changed over the centuries.

This is the difficulty for Wesley and anyone else in historic restoration: there is just no way to know how much the colonial collard was like any collard available today. The same is true for all garden vegetables: changing insect and disease pressures have caused plants to evolve; indeed the plants, their pollinators, and their pests continually coevolve over the years. Soil types, weather extremes, and general climate conditions also vary over both time and region. No aspect of the environment is static, so plants cannot be static. "We can approximate the early collard, using selection practices that 'reverse' the changes, modifying the plant to earlier forms," says Greene, "but even if we use seventeenth-century paintings and descriptions, the plant isn't quite the same."

Perhaps a key factor is Western European climate. In areas where the collard first developed along shores of France and England, climates are not at all like those of the southern United States. In its Old World environments, the collard found cool, mild winters and ideal conditions for seed saving. The plant that could be selected for height (ultimately reaching twelve feet in the varieties grown in the Channel Islands, between England and France) or longevity (living four or five years, producing tasty leaves all the while) was unable to make those adaptations in the South's greater annual temperature fluctuations and longer droughts.

In fact, seed-saving practices commonly failed in the first American colonial gardens because plants and gardeners were both facing such new climate and soil conditions. European vegetable seed, mainly from England or the Netherlands, was imported by informal means and commercial venture. Gardening experts of the eighteenth century noted that American-saved seed would not do for most vegetables, saying that the plants would not thrive, or would produce only poor comestibles. These writers often understood that the climate contrast was a factor, but they had not developed good plant breeding methods, and seed propagation was still mostly unscientific.

Over a few generations of seed saving and selective effort, however, locally adapted plants were developed that did thrive in the South; this included the collard, one of which may have been the Green Glaze. This plant was reported as having excellent resistance to cabbage worms (called collard worms in parts of the South). These worms, introduced from Europe, could easily destroy a crop almost as soon as American gardens were planted, so any varieties that seemed less attractive to these worms would be celebrated. The supposed reason for the superior resistance of Green Glaze is in its surface texture, which is smoother and shinier than other collards, thus the name. Entomologists claim there is a tendency for cabbage butterflies to avoid shinier leaves, but just why they do, no one knows.

The features of Green Glaze distinguish the greens from the other collards being grown. Contemporary writers refer to other early collard forms by the names "blue collard," "long collard," and "long-foot collard." Were they more like a kale? Some experts seem to think so, since kale is a nonheading form of *Brassica oleracea*. But Dr. Mark Farnham, a geneticist with the USDA's Vegetable Laboratory, has tested the DNA of collards, kales, and cabbages and concludes that collards should not be confused with kale, despite the fact that both are nonheading. According to Dr. Farnham, "They are all very closely related, but now we believe that collards are more akin to cabbage than to kale."

We must turn to the Old World if we are to complete our story, for collards are an Old World vegetable. In his history of Virginia, Captain John Smith made an appropriate observation: "as Geography without History seemeth a carkasse without motion, so History without Geography wandreth as a Vagrant without a certain habitation."[2] A historical geography of collards will explain where they came from and how they got to the American South.

The Origins and Diffusion of the Collard

If collards were common in the southern United States by 1820, where had they come from? Could the collard plant be native to the American continent? After all, more collards are grown in the American South today than anywhere else in the world, and the collard has some of the appearance (some would say even the taste) of a wild plant. Could it have been brought from tropical Africa? There are collards grown today in parts of Africa, and several other Southern foods, such as okra, originated in Africa. What about Portugal or its Brazilian New World colony, the two key countries outside the South where a plant almost identical to the collard is popular?

An Old World Origin

To those who are familiar with it, the collard plant seems deeply attached to the South. As few people outside the South respect it or desire it, and the weather in the South seems to match its needs, many Southerners we asked believe it is indigenous.

The possibility of a New World origin, however, was quickly eliminated. The ancestor of the collard is not native to the Americas. In fact, North American botanists find no native populations of any relatives of the *Brassicaceae* family. There is also no evidence that Native Americans grew domestic forms of the plant prior to contact with European invaders. This does not mean there are no escapees in the landscape: you may discover a "wild" collard or cabbage on the edge of a field on the Gulf Coast's sandy plain. Sometimes, where the microclimate is mild, the seeds of a garden collard become established and will initiate a small population of refugees. Such occurrences are rare though, for the plant is not truly adapted to wild Southern climates and instead generally clings to the pampered conditions of a tended garden.

Where Europe faces the Atlantic, however, you will find the wild plant *Brassica oleracea* var. *oleracea* growing in widely scattered—but related—populations (see map 4). It grows only on or near seaside cliffs along the northern shores of Spain, the western shore of France, the southern coast of Britain, the Channel Islands, and the Frisian Islands off the shores of the Netherlands.[3] A number of populations of the plant still exist along the rocky shores of the Mediterranean, but early colonial America saw very few migrants from that seacoast. This grayish-green wild plant has smaller leaves than any adult cabbage or collard, and more of its mass is devoted to the tall flower stalk (up to four feet on ideal sites). The flowers themselves do not vary much: four small petals arranged in a cross about ¼ inch in diameter, in white, yellow, or somewhere in between.[4]

Walk away from these cliffs to nearby towns and villages and you encounter many home gardens with domestic cabbages and kales. Today, there are thousands of gardens within close range of the wild plant, and there must have been many in ancient times as well. Somewhere along these highly humanized coastal lands, probably in many independent cases, the human domestication of *Brassica oleracea* occurred, perhaps three thousand years ago.

Can we narrow this down to a smaller area? Only by conjecture, given the barrier of so many centuries, but there is a chance that we can eliminate Britain as the earliest site for domestication. One botanist has collected evidence that none of the wild populations in Britain are native. Ecologist Dr. Neil Mitchell has inventoried all reports in Britain of the wild *Brassica oleracea* and finds most were or are in close proximity of gardens of domestic cabbage or sea bird nesting areas.[5] Although wild forms were reported in the first published floras and *Brassica oleracea* was common in Britain at least 500 years ago, even these were in places (e.g., Dover) where they could have escaped from cultivation. To support his conclusion, Mitchell offers documented modern examples of escape. In certain maritime microclimates of Southern Britain, the domestic Brassica plants are able to become established outside the protection of human hands. For example, Mitchell quotes the early botanist Syme as observing in 1863 that "red cabbage of neglected gardens at the seaside pass back in a few generations to the condition of the wild cabbage." Furthermore, many of the wild populations are in decline, or have disappeared over time, which suggests they are not competitively successful with native vegetation. Seabirds are recognized as important vectors for the dispersal of seed, either carrying the seed in the mud on their feet or in their gut in undigested form. Many wild plant populations are close to seabird nesting areas. Therefore, Mitchell concludes that the wild *Brassica oleracea* is an introduced species and not native to Britain.

Such assessments are lacking for France, the Channel Islands, the Frisian Islands, and Spain; but among these, the region with the most stable wild plant populations is northern Spain.[6] Since these multiple populations are apparently competitive in their plant communities, they are more likely to be indigenous. Perhaps the earliest steps toward *Brassica* domestication occurred in this area.

How, then, did the wild plant become domestic? Most scholars believe that the gathering of wild plants shifted from simple protection to more specialized care, until seeds, seedlings, or cuttings were gathered and propagated in gardens.[7] The young leaves of wild *Brassica oleracea*, although bitter, are edible and nutritious, and available during winter and spring in their native range. The reaping of relatively high nutritional content needs little human energy input, justifying the choice to collect and eat wild edible greens for subsistence. Even today, the weeds collected by traditional cultures are often young plants that sprout in disturbed environments, such as newly cleared fields and field edges.

Thus, the domestication of collards, which in this case is defined as the incorporation of the plant into diets and then gardens, may have begun where they were first weed species among cultivated crops near the shore.[8] Such weeds might have been left in the field for weeks and then removed as a kind of first crop before they could negatively affect the main crop. Eventually, the seeds of mature plants on field edges were collected and sown in their own plots, where further selection would produce the many modern varieties. A number of food plants eventually developed from *Brassica oleracea*. A tough plant adapted to such a harsh environment is impressive, but that may have also been its advantage: this plant is adaptable and superior to many leafy greens in its ability to grow slowly and to store nutrients.[9]

By the time there were written records, about the first century AD in Rome, the domestic *Brassica oleracea* had been transformed from its collard-like ancestral shape into at least three forms: heading, nonheading, and edible-stem.[10] Broccoli and cauliflower appear to have been developed somewhat later in the northeastern Mediterranean.[11] Even today plant explorers are discovering local broccoli varieties being preserved by seed savers in Italy, a testament to the richness of the *Brassica oleracea* domestication.[12] The collard and kale were (and still are) two versions of the nonheading form. The main difference between them seems to be in their cold hardiness. Most kales were apparently selected for a short growing season and tolerance of rather cold conditions.

The Medieval Colewort and the Collard

Through those many unrecorded centuries of cultivated selection, various parts of the plant (leaves, stem, and inflorescence) were encouraged to store even more nutrients. Human goals were gradually reflected in about a dozen distinct forms scattered around Western Europe. Several heading varieties are mentioned in Spain around the year 1150.[13] A depiction of a plant called "caulis onati," which has all the characteristics of our Southern collard, was included in *Tacuinum Sanitatis,* an illustrated manuscript about garden plants first produced in Lombardy, Italy, in the 14th century (see fig. 22). Mark Farnham, a Brassica expert, believes the leaf shape, stem length, size, and color indicate a plant quite like the modern Southern collard.

In the year 1354, a gardener for the Rotherhithe palace in southern England purchased 20 pounds of colewort seed, enough to sow two acres.[14] Was this colewort similar to what we have today in the southern United States? Prior to 1500 we have no depictions or clear descriptions of domesticated *Brassica oleracea,* but a painting by Pieter Brueghel the Younger in about 1530 gives us an excellent glimpse of one form common at that time. The painting shows the Low Country (Netherlands) landscape in winter. In a snow-laden village, peasants go about their daily routines: carrying a load, repairing a fence, hunting birds, chatting with neighbors. There is a small wattle-and-daub hut, perhaps ten by fifteen feet, and beside it an old woman is tending her garden, only about seven by seven feet. In this fenced garden are seven *Brassica oleracea* plants, each about two feet tall and a foot and a half across, from which some leaves have been harvested. Sylvia Landsberg, a scholar of medieval gardens, calls these "coleworts" and says the closest plant to these still in existence is the Southern collard.[15]

Landsberg's correlation of the medieval European colewort with the Southern collard seems reasonable. The plants cannot be the same, for the Southern collard has undergone many centuries of adaptation to its own environment. But the collard—that is, the old open-pollinated forms, not recent hybrids—is more primitive than other domesticated forms of *Brassica oleracea.* Its structure is most like that of the ancient form: the flower, stalk, and horizontal loose leaves very much resemble the same shape as those of wild collard. It has high levels of glucosinolate, a compound that makes the wild form bitter, but which modern domestication has "bred down" to one fourth or less of the original level.[16] And the collard is tolerant of a range of cold, heat, and drought. Old varieties tolerate lows of 18 degrees Fahrenheit (only kale can tolerate lower temperatures) and highs of 100 degrees Fahrenheit.[17] As with most organisms, the more refined plants are less likely to be tolerant of extreme conditions. So the collard is relatively similar to the ancestral wild plant from which it was developed. For this reason, we believe it is a direct descendant of the medieval European colewort—itself quite similar to the wild ancestor.

With the colewort well established in Western Europe by 1530 and its descendant the collard established across the Atlantic by 1820, the bridge across those 300 intervening years has four possibilities. The Southern collard could have come from the following:

- Africa, along the routes of the slave trade
- Portugal or Brazil with settlers to South Carolina, Georgia, and Florida
- Spain, with settlers to Florida, Georgia, and South Carolina
- Britain, with settlers to the thirteen American colonies

These possibilities all begin with the likelihood that by 1500 the colewort/collard was widely grown in Western Europe and, therefore, could have been transferred by many paths across the Atlantic.

Could Collards Have Arrived via Africa?

A most fascinating possibility is that African slaves introduced collards to the Southern colonies, and there is wide support for this theory. At least twenty sources have proposed an African origin, including academic and popular books, journal articles, newspapers, historic gardens, and websites. The most notable proponent of this theory is historian John Egerton, whose widely read work *Southern Food: At Home, On the Road, In History* asserts, "from Africa with the people in bondage came new foods: okra, black-eyed peas, collard greens, yams, benne seed, and watermelons."[18] The *Encyclopedia of Food and Culture*, a leading reference edited by Solomon Katz, states that "the greens of the southeastern United States—collard greens, kale and mustard greens—have their roots in Africa."[19] Many newspaper and magazine stories repeat the claim. The *Seattle Times* states, "the okra, collard greens, and sweet potatoes . . . found on many Charleston restaurant menus came in the seventeenth century with the slaves brought from Africa."[20]

The foremost authority on American foods of African origins is the University of California, Los Angeles, geographer Judith Carney, who demonstrated that Africans played the lead role in establishing rice production in South Carolina. Her book *Black Rice* makes an excellent case for the technological skills of African farmers, without which white plantation owners could not have succeeded.[21] With her more recent book *In the Shadow of Slavery*, she and Richard Rosomoff sought out the range of plants and farming skills that African women and men brought to the Americas during the slavery era. The plants introduced from Africa include some of the most important plants still being grown in tropical America (including Central America and the northern two-thirds of South America): rice, yams, millet, cola nuts, sesame, sorghum, plantains, taro, watermelon, okra, pepper, and coffee.

This list of New World introductions from Africa does not, however, include collards. What Carney and Rosomoff did find was that other cooked greens were central to many African meals, particularly in the Caribbean and tropical South America, where African influence remains the strongest. Perhaps this is credited to the tropical ecosystems of the western hemisphere being a closer match to those of Africa.

Yet, we feel that an African source for American collards is a possibility. There were long centuries of opportunity between ancient Rome and America's colonial era, a window of time when Western European *Brassica oleracea* forms might have found their way to Sub-Saharan Africa and from there on to the New World. One reason to suspect an African origin is that collards are grown commercially today in seven African countries: Angola, Ethiopia, Kenya, Liberia, Mozambique, Nigeria, and South Africa. Off the coast of West Africa, collards are also grown in the Cape Verde Islands and São Tomé.[22]

Ecological requirements, however, seem to make an African origin improbable. Unlike the African-origin plants—such as yams, rice, and okra—the collard is a cool-season crop, usually planted in summer and harvested in late fall and early winter. Otherwise, as it matures, the plant suffers from pest problems and summer's high evapotranspiration rates. Collards will suffer in extended high heat or drought, their leaves becoming desiccated and less useful as a food source.[23] As explained earlier, *Brassica oleracea* plants require a winter season to produce seed. Traditional (that is, seed saving) collard gardeners are, thus, constrained to places with a true winter. Such conditions are not found in the African slave-source regions—that is, the broad coastal region from Senegal to Cameroon, as well as Angola, Tanzania, and Mozambique.[24]

Modern peoples, even in poor areas of Africa, often have access to imported seeds today. Could Sub-Saharan Africans, during the slave-trade era, have grown collards from regularly imported seed? There might have been an early cross-Saharan vegetable seed trade, but it seems unlikely that African villagers would have traded long distance for something as nonessential as collard seed. Africans had at hand many native plants already providing green leaves for cooking. Botanical studies of Africa show that communities have traditionally eaten hundreds of different native leafy greens,[25] and the most widely used leafy green plants are of the amaranth family.

If collards were indeed adopted in Africa and then carried by slaves to America, we would expect to find some reference to the plant being useful well before 1800. So we reviewed records from the slave-trade era of the useful plants of Sub-Saharan Africa. European explorers in the 1700s made reports on plants with potential for medicine, food staples, luxury foods, and industrial applications.[26] We could find no record of *Brassica* species grown in Sub-Saharan Africa prior to 1830.[27] We also reviewed modern inventories of Africa's useful plants—all of these identify *Brassica oleracea* varieties as recent introductions from Europe.[28]

So, what explains the fact that collards and cabbage are being grown in Africa today? There are small highland zones in Kenya and Ethiopia, and especially the Jos Plateau region of northern Nigeria, where "winter" temperatures are cool enough to cause flowering in *Brassica* species. Cabbage and collards are grown today by Africans in these areas for both export and local consumption. This explains the modern Kenyan and Ethiopian collards. What about Angola, Cape Verde, and Mozambique? In each case, sources indicate that the plants were introduced in the late nineteenth century to serve immigrant European populations.[29]

European settlers have, in the past century or so, transformed African cultures, and introduced European food preferences.[30] Since the early twentieth century, colonial wars, ethnic conflicts, and economic stress have sent many rural Africans into cities, a massive migration that has disrupted traditional ties to the land and facilitated—even forced—a shift in diets.[31] Whereas people once gathered from the wild and from field edges the more nutritious native greens, according to African nutritionists, today there is a booming demand for domesticated cabbage.[32] African plant resource specialists have noted for thirty years a loss of native food plants from local diets in part due to this shift to introduced foods, such as white bread and cabbage.[33]

Liberia, the one West African country where collards are reportedly popular, provides an ironic exception. It was colonized between 1820 and 1860 by hundreds of freed slaves, mostly from Mississippi, who brought an Americanized culture *into* Africa and seem to have avoided cultural integration with the Africans whom they displaced. Indeed, in 1830, one Liberian settler wrote home to supporters in Mississippi requesting collard seed.[34] It seems the only collards being grown in Liberia were in the gardens of former slaves from the American South. And today, in twentieth century Liberia, collards are said to be widely grown.

Curious to learn firsthand about West African vegetable production, we carried out field work in Ghana in January 2005 and found cultivation of white cabbage. In the markets, cabbage as well as a number of native leafy greens collected from roadside shrubs, trees, and herbaceous plants were available for sale. But no market sellers, farmers, or seed dealers were familiar with collards. Even cabbage was recognized as a recent import and only profitable as a crop since the 1980s. It seems West African cabbage growers face severe pest problems.[35] A University of Ghana botanist explained that Brassica plants are not well adapted to the tropical climate and only thrive under continual pesticide sprayings and irrigation.[36]

The African vector still is not disproved, for—in spite of these constraints—much about the food in Africa during the early European colonial era is unknown. There may have been some successful introduction of collards from Africa to America via slave ships which embarked for America with collard seeds on board. We have not ruled out this possibility; indeed, we hold out hope that if collard seed were transported in this fashion, we'll one day discover some documentary evidence of it.

From Portugal or Brazil?

What about Portugal as a source for the collards adopted in the American South? This theory seems more plausible for several reasons. First, the *Brassica oleracea* grown in Portugal (variety *costata*) for many centuries is nearly identical to southern collards[37] (see figure 23).

During the 1700s, there were several hundred Portuguese immigrants to South Carolina, Georgia, and Florida. Most went to Charlestown (Charleston) by 1750, and it is likely some would have had vegetable gardens planted with *Brassica oleracea* seeds brought directly from Portugal. The British plant record indicates that Portuguese collards were being grown in Britain as early as 1820, so we know that British people were open to adopting this form of *Brassica oleracea*. A diffusion from Portuguese gardens seems possible, since seed from Europe was in great demand by Southern colonists throughout this early period.

But this theory has problems. The number of families that emigrated to South Carolina was only in the dozens, and their exchanges with English immigrants in the colonies were somewhat limited. Perhaps Portuguese settlements in Brazil provided a kind of halfway station from which adoption in the Southern colonies could have been facilitated. After all, some travelers as early as 1669 mention a form of cabbage being cultivated in Brazil.[38] Collards (a form from Brazil classified as *Brassica oleracea var. costata*) are grown today in gardens throughout Brazil, and southern Brazil has sufficient winter weather to force a collard plant into flowering and seed production. The old Brazilian tradition of eating Portuguese collards is well known. This cultural trait could have been transferred to North America prior to 1820. There is an interesting connection between southerners and Brazil: slave traders often called at ports in both regions, and business partnerships linked them in the late 1700s. Then, as the Civil War ended in 1865, a group of Confederates emigrated from the South to Brazil rather than submit to the Union government and possible penalties. It is interesting to imagine them reminiscing about the Old South as they enjoyed bowls of Portuguese collards (*Brassica oleracea* var. *costata*). Perhaps some Brazilian seed was carried to the southern United States for selling and/or sharing. Exchange of garden seed between English and Portuguese settlers was probably too limited and maybe too late to explain widespread adoption throughout the English-speaking southern colonies, however. We have found no record to support this conjecture. Still, we must allow the possibility that Portuguese collard seed made some minor contribution to the collard germplasm of the US South.

From Spain?

Collards are mentioned in a number of reports as Caribbean food plants, although never as a common plant. A 1925 report of collards being grown in the former Spanish colony of Puerto Rico exists.[39] A garden plant called the "long-foot cabbage" was reported in Montserrat by geographer David Thomasson in 1994, apparently an heirloom that could have old Spanish antecedents.[40] The Spanish have a long history of remaking the Caribbean landscape. On the island of Hispaniola, for instance, the Spanish were planting

European crops as early as about 1500.[41] One plant historian concludes that Spanish explorer Giovanni Battista Benzoni found cabbages thriving on Hispaniola in 1565. Collards could well have been in those gardens. In the 1600s and early 1700s European ships began to carry sauerkraut for preventing scurvy; therefore, it is possible that cabbages and even collards were planted for just such a purpose. Unfortunately, we have few documents of the vegetable gardens from that period, partly because greens were seldom considered important for investment or documentation. Instead, it was more common for Spanish colonists to steal food from Native Americans— maize, corn, and beans being considered poor but acceptable substitutes for the foods of Spain, and theft being preferable to growing one's own crops.[42] Cabbages were certainly grown, and collards were probably grown as well, for they might better tolerate the heat.[43] But the tropical climate there would, as in Africa, limit the plant to the gardens of the small elite who could afford fresh vegetable seed imported from Europe.

Because there is a possibility that the peach tree, popular in Spain, was introduced to the South by Spanish colonists, there is also some possibility that collards were introduced through the same pathway. Hernando de Soto led some 600 men through the American South between 1539 and 1542. Then, as early as the 1600s, various European settlers encountered peach trees in Native American villages.[44] Perhaps the collard was also being spread at this time. However, the necessary logic is rather strained, with records suggesting that because de Soto's army planned to plunder most of their food, they carried no fresh vegetables and, as far as we know, planted no gardens. Cabbage or collard seed would certainly seem an unlikely cargo for these conquistadors with gold on their minds.

There is yet another intriguing possibility. Trade and cultural exchange between Native Americans and Spanish peoples did take place throughout the colonial period.[45] In the 1520s, coastal South Carolina—where collards would one day be quite popular—was host to a Spanish colony at the mouth of the Pee Dee River. Here the Spaniards landed and captured seventy Native Americans in the year 1520. By 1526, ships arrived from Europe with

a full settlement of approximately 500 Spanish men and women, 100 enslaved Africans, and some native "interpreters."[46] Vegetable gardens of the
time could have included coleworts (there are records of such gardens). But
the settlement experiment was short-lived. The colonists suffered from terrible disease, hunger, and dissent. Within a year, the Spanish settlers had to
be rescued and transported to Hispaniola, and the surviving African slaves
fled to join local Native American tribes. In this last event we see the potential for collards to have been introduced at the juncture of Spanish, African,
and Native American cultures. Perhaps someone in that group took collard
seed and shared it with others. But these people left us no record of their
lives, much less their choice of food plants. The chance of this colony serving as one vector for the Southern collard is slender, but not impossible.

From Britain?

What about the possibility that the Southern collard derives from British
plants? Is there a clear link between early modern Britain to the American
colonies?

The *Oxford English Dictionary* (OED) says *collard* is a corruption of
colewort.[47] The first printed record of such a corruption occurs in England
in 1755. The word *collard* shows up again in England in 1807, this time
as interchangeable with *colewort* in R. W. Dickson's *Practical Agriculture*.[48]
A London grocer advertised the sale of collards along with cabbages and
turnips in 1823.[49] This appearance suggests the continued presence of the
term—and the plant—in common parlance. The word *collard* is identified
as meaning colewort in an 1850 list of Britain's archaic words.[50] An 1881 list
of Oxfordshire words includes *collets* as an archaic word for small spring
cabbages, and an 1888 list for Berkshire, England, says young cabbages
were once called "colluts."[51] Our search of primary documents turned up
these early American examples in print of the words *collard*, *collards*, and
collerds:

> 1781: "The negroes here raise great quantities of . . . collerds. They
> have no cabbages here."[52]
> 1793: "a small garden for peas, bean, collards and other . . ."[53]

1796: "They made beans, ground peas, cymblins, gourds, watermelons, collards and onions."[54]

1814: "Micajah Benge's collard and potato patch, comprising about two acres."[55]

1818: "In the garden they cultivate their collards, i.e., probably coleworts."[56]

1822: "seed for colewort or collard $1.50 per lb." (seed catalog).[57]

1830: "One patch of collards and one patch of turnips" (named in a will).[58]

These examples seem to confirm the early American use of *collard* to mean *colewort*. A fascinating record of the words *collard* and *colewort* is found in the diary kept by a wealthy woman in eastern North Carolina during the 1830s and 1840s. Eliza Person Mitchell recorded her daily gardening activities in Warren County between 1833 and 1844. She mentions planting coleworts and cabbage in 1833, 1835, and again on March 7, 1837. Two days later, on March 9, she writes that she "sowed collard seed." She mentions planting collards (and cabbages, so she is not conflating those two) annually every year after, never again writing *colewort*. If she were alive today, we could ask her to confirm, but it seems likely she was simply adopting a different, more phonetic spelling, rather than changing plants in midseason.

Combining these examples with those in the OED, it seems clear that *colewort* was pronounced "collard" by people in England and America before the new more informal spelling was adopted.[59] If we are correct, many or most "colewort" mentions are actually mentions of collards, at least beginning in the late 1700s.

Are Southern Collards Actually Descended from European Coleworts?

To confirm a direct link between colewort in Europe and collard in the US South, we must first find good descriptions of the colewort during the critical window of diffusion. Sometime between 1530 and 1830, a significant amount of colewort seed had to make the Atlantic crossing. There must be a logical explanation for that. Secondly, there should be early descriptions of the Southern collard. If these match the plants identified as available from Europe, then there is a reasonable case that southern collards came primarily from Britain.

Commercial seed production in England was relatively minor prior to 1640. Still, there was a trade in seed for coleworts, leeks, and onions, apparently the leading garden vegetables of medieval Britain.[60] Seed trade expanded in the century after 1660 to support the expansion of arable acres, mainly in the southeastern counties.[61] The majority of British gardeners were seed savers at that time, because they could not afford to do otherwise.[62] But with the enclosures and the industrialization of farms from the mid-1700s, rural traditions began to dissipate.

However, across the sea, gardening was on the increase through the 1700s, and British American colonists were regularly importing nearly all their garden seed from Britain.[63] This situation developed because the colonists preferred the foods they had known in the mother country and also because they were unable to produce all the seed they needed in the New World.[64] Seed saving depends on having a plant well adjusted to its soil and climate. Otherwise, the plant will not produce much viable seed, so imported seed was in high demand. An early example of domestic seed production was Martha Logan of Charleston, South Carolina, who grew and sold garden seed as early as 1754, including cabbage and colewort seed.[65] But, in general, America's commercial seed producers would not arrive on the scene until about 1800, so there was free reign for British (and Dutch) firms until that time to exploit the American need.[66]

Based on the above conditions, it seems logical that, prior to 1800, British colewort seed arrived in significant quantities in American ports, commercially and as gifts among family and friends. Confirming the commercial flow are numerous seed advertisements in American colonial newspapers that regularly included "colewort" seed for sale.[67] Determining how the seeds were shared is more difficult to ascertain. We searched for but could not find specific cases where colewort/collard seed was shared from Britain to the American South, but it is generally known that seed saving and sharing were widespread traditions.[68]

The earliest definitive plant descriptions in England are by John Gerard, whose famous *Herbal* of 1633 describes sixteen and illustrates twelve different "coleworts" or *Brassica* plants.[69] This publication appeared before systematic plant taxonomy, so Gerard's scientific names do not match modern ones. Here are a few of the *Brassicas* he includes:

Garden Colewort: *Brassica vulgaris sativa*

Curled Garden Cole: *Brassica sativa crispa*

Red Colewort: *Brassica rubra*

White Cabbage Cole: *Brassica capitata alba*

Red Cabbage Cole: *Brassica capitata rubra*

Cole-Florie: *Brassica florida*

The first one on Gerard's list, Garden Colewort, appears to be the closest to what we know today as a collard. The description is as follows: "The Garden Colewort hath a great many broad leaves of a deepe blacke greene colour, mixed with ribs and lines of reddish and white colours; the stalke groweth out of the middle of the leaves, branched with sundry armes bearing at the top little yellow floures."[70] This description sounds more colorful than the typical Southern collard, but our experience is that many heirloom varieties grown today in the South have these colors. Color is one of the most unstable characteristics of the species. You may recall our discovery of Charlie Malone's and Mac Walter's purple collards in Alabama. These plants could easily be expressing ancient English traits.

Further evidence of similarity with the Southern collard is found in Gerard's description of the garden culture; he says that the best time to sow these coleworts is in September and the time to eat the leaves is in winter "when they are fittest."[71] This scenario is very close to the garden tradition for Southern collards. Almost a century later, in England, we have Philip Miller's 1759 reference book *The Gardeners Dictionary*, which contrasts common coleworts and cabbages, declaring "the common Colewort, or Dorsetshire Kale, is now almost lost near London, where their Markets are usually supplied with Cabbage Plants, instead of them; and these being tenderer, and more delicate, in Winter are much more cultivated than the common

Colewort, which is better able to resist the cold in sever Winters, than those, but is not near so delicate till pinched by Frost. And since the Winters in England have been generally temperate of late Years, the common Cabbage Plants have constantly been cultivated by the Gardeners near London, and sold in the Markets as Coleworts, . . . Indeed, where Farmers sow Coleworts to feed their Milch-cattle in the Spring, when there is a Scarcity of Herbage, the common Colewort is to be preferred, as being so hardy that no Frost will destroy it."[72] Miller's description of the "common colewort" lacks detail on the plant's form, but it seems to be similar to both Gerard's garden colewort and the Southern collard: nonheading and hardier than cabbage, a flavor improved by frost, and considered distinct from its cousin the kale. Given that England's climate was and is more moderate in both winter and summer than that of the Southern United States, any colewort seed raised in Britain would have made a rather poor match when planted across the Atlantic. There was likely a high rate of failure for much colewort seed in the early colonial years. Gradually, however, successful gardens would derive from selections made year by year, until coleworts (now called collards) became better adapted to the southern American climate, soils, and pests.

We believe there is a distinguishable match between the British colewort and the southern collard, but there is a twist in Miller's description: this common colewort was in decline by 1759—at least around London—and fell to apparent extinction by about 1920. This result seems shocking for a country that just two centuries prior honored the colewort as a fairly popular garden plant.[73] Taking its place was its own genetic progeny, the cabbage, which by the 1870s is being described as ubiquitous.[74] Perhaps the shift toward cabbages was hastened by the industrial revolution and its resulting urbanization. As villages and rural areas were emptied, the rural gardens were fewer in number, while demand for fresh vegetables in cities dramatically increased. The shipment and storage of coleworts was at that time rather impractical, while heading cabbages would have been ideal. Coleworts were being used as spring fodder, and it is not surprising that they eventually fell out of favor. Had there been no outlet for the colewort—a new role as the Southern collard—this old plant might have been lost altogether.

Just as American collards were becoming widespread and consumed by southerners, they seem to have been abandoned in the very country from which they were most likely derived. Nonheading forms of *Brassica oleracea* may be inconvenient for commerce, but they have four distinct advantages over cabbage: 1) they are generally more nutritious; 2) their open structure harbors fewer insect and fungal pests; 3) they tolerate heat better, hotter conditions being a more common challenge in the U.S. South than in Britain; and 4) they can be harvested a few leaves at a time, allowing a more judicious use of garden space in winter. Finally, some of the flavor of collards must have found a niche in the southern palate, for in spite of its debasement by many, this old plant retains millions of fans today—perhaps more than it ever had in medieval Europe.

In summation, the most likely mode of introduction for collard seeds to the southern United States was by a wide number of British settlers, bringing seeds that would have produced collards varying in height, color, and hardiness. The Southern collard in certain quarters may also have some ancestry that was borne over the Atlantic by Spanish and/or Portuguese settlers and possibly on African slave ships. Regardless of the plant's origin, in the hands of primarily African American gardeners and cooks, collards became a classic Southern food, often paired with cornbread, barbecued pork, and black-eyed peas.

8

Mapping the Southern Collard
Core and Domain

The Southern collard culture region has a central core and a broader domain, concepts that were made popular by historical geographer Donald Meinig and that represent two levels of intensity in a cultural practice. The core is that region where the practice is most common, or even dominant, and the domain is the region where the practice is influential, but less dominant. In this case, the collard core is where collards are the dominant source for cooked greens, and the domain is where collards are essentially codominant with turnip greens, mustard greens, or both.

A fair part of the South is not really collard country, having few collard patches or collard lovers, lying outside either the core or the domain. Tennessee, for example, is a state where collards are seldom found. Turnip greens are the dominant cooked greens there, as they are in Kentucky and West Virginia. These states have a lesser commitment to cooked greens of any kind, although there are always some individual collard fans there. Another part of the noncollard South is northern Virginia. Although the major grocery stores offer collards in their produce sections, the managers tell us that sales are low, and home collard patches are quite rare. Edna Lewis, a nationally known African American chef born in Freetown, Orange County, Virginia, a community founded by her grandfather and his friends shortly after their emancipation, was raised in the kitchen and knows much about her family's food traditions. However, Lewis says that until she was grown she "didn't even know there was such a thing as collard greens."[1]

Parts of nine Southern states lie in the region we have designated as the collard domain, which includes a small area in southern Arkansas and northern Louisiana, easternmost Louisiana, southern and eastern Mississippi, most of Alabama, northern Florida, and the piedmonts of Georgia, the Carolinas, and Virginia. Southerners in the collard domain may grow up in a family that favors collards or even a community or county where collards are common. But collard intensity there did not cover enough area or enough people to be picked up by our field observations or by our surveys of extension agents, down-home restaurants, produce managers, college students, or seed retailers. Following is analysis of data and details discovered in key parts of those nine states.

ALABAMA'S BLACK BELT

Like a wide grin from ear to ear, the Black Belt sweeps across the middle of Alabama, lapping into Mississippi and Georgia on either side. It's a region named for its dark, organically rich soil that drew wealthy cotton planters beginning in the 1820s. After the Civil War, this region held a major concentration of sharecroppers, still growing cotton. Most were former slaves and their descendants. These small farm families—black and white—suffered exploitation by large landowners, decimation by boll weevils, and, finally, soil exhaustion. Finally defeated, the majority of rural people got out, fleeing to the cities as soon as they could afford a bus ticket.

As recently as the 1960s, however, the Black Belt was still home to many sharecropper families scratching out a hard life. The rural poor were painfully visible then, and the national "War on Poverty" program sent in social workers to help. Nancy Scheper-Hughes was one such helper, who went to Wilcox County in 1967 to help survey more than 900 black share-cropper families. In her words, "we uncovered a ravaged population often living on the edges of starvation and largely dependent for survival on ca-pricious federal farm programs, families who went hungry during the lean winter and early spring months with meals comprised of starch, sugar, and fat—that is, grits, biscuits, cornbread, peanut butter, fried bologna, fatback, Kool-Aid, and coffee." But one asset from their cultural heritage played an essential role in their survival: mustard and collard greens. Were it not for these vitamin-rich leaves, she wrote, the sharecroppers' health would have been far worse.[2]

The sharecroppers' fields of the Black Belt have now been replaced by large pastures for beef cattle, catfish ponds, and fields of soybeans and cot-ton. Large old planters' houses, well maintained by descendants, are still spaced along the main roads, usually fronted by pecan orchards; but small farms are quite rare, and most people are clustered into towns and cities such as Selma and Montgomery. There are very few winter gardens among the sparse rural population that remains.

Interviews of local stores' employees, especially produce managers in the grocery stores, yielded the information that, although all three greens—collard, mustard, and turnip—are consumed in Alabama's Black Belt, col-lards are the most popular. Many people spoke of mixing collards with tur-nip or mustard greens. This is one region of Alabama where restaurants consistently feature collard greens. In a stretch from Livingston (Sumter County) on the western border to Tuskegee (Macon County) in the east, nine restaurants offer no other type of greens but collards. The Alabama Black Belt was the *only* place in the Deep South where we found such con-sistent restaurant offerings.

NORTHERN FLORIDA

Florida is a state so modified by late twentieth-century immigrants that solid areas of food traditions are hard to find, even in most of its northern parts. Digging into the past, however, we found a long history of collard culture in northern Florida:

1825: Tallahassee newspaper says cabbages and collards are "seldom seen in market."[3]

1846: In Leon County, Charles Bannerman's plantation had a garden of collards and turnips.

1874: A newspaper in Polk County includes a story of some large local collards.

1889: A writer from Pasco County says turnips and collards are both popular.

1900: Writer Zora Neale Hurston says she loved collards growing up in Orange County.

1921: Alachua County's turpentine camps have collards in the garden.

1935: WPA writer reports that Jackson County's black families usually raise collards.

1950s: Poet Cornelius Eady loved the collards at his mother's Gainesville home place.[4]

In Florida's Panhandle, on the back roads, we found some nice collard patches. One of the larger ones was in Esto, just half a mile south of the Alabama line. Down a side road there is a collard booth, where customers are trusted to leave money for the collards they take out of a bucket (see fig. 25). On several other occasions we have seen additional instances of collards sold on the honor system. A garden of collards sits close by a highway without fencing. A handmade sign attracts the customer: "Collards, You Pick." Usually there is a table, and on the table is a knife for cutting the fibrous collard stems and a box or coffee can. All this is usually under an open shed. Next to the can there will be a note, saying something like "take what you need . . . put money in can." These little business ventures thrive only in marginal remnants of the South where trust is still a tangible character of the people.

GEORGIA

Atlanta is the country's ninth most populous metropolitan area, making it a geographical force in the South, especially in North Georgia. This collection of twenty-eight counties with well over five million people, covering nearly 8,400 square miles, has far more sprawl than Miami (the Southeast's largest metro area, by a slim margin). In fact, since only about 8 percent of those five million people actually live inside the Atlanta city limits, this metro area's suburban network is vast.

Navigating these suburbs over a couple of days, we found comfort food in good restaurants. More places in Atlanta serve collards than anywhere else. Could it be that collards provide an important "post-rural" comfort for the millions who fled the rural and small town South? Maybe the *average* Atlantan today is at least two generations removed from authentic country collards, cut fresh from the farm's home garden, but food memory seems to cross generations. Perhaps in a dish of collards, the preurban Georgia survives. The vast Atlanta metropolitan area is not included in the collard core, because there are so few collard gardens and so much diversity in the produce managers' reports on sales of greens. Atlanta has seen a century of significant immigration from beyond the South and is perhaps farther from a homogenous food culture than any other part of the South.

The Collard Core

The southern limit of the collard core is in the southeastern rural districts of Georgia. Drive around the back roads near Augusta and Savannah, and you will see many people raising collards; go into restaurants, and you meet many collard lovers.

The connection between Georgia and collards could be seen as simply a part of popular culture. For example, a speech by Methodist bishop Earl Hunt declared that for early Methodists, "sin is as basic as life itself and as common as collards in Georgia."[5] Does this derive from the widely used plant variety called the "Georgia collard"? Maybe the bishop could have said "As common as turnips in Tennessee"? That simile would have been just as accurate.

At the University of West Georgia in Carroll County, a 2009 dinner celebrating the regional foods of "Piedmont Georgia" featured collard greens. In Chatham County, just upriver from Savannah, the small suburban community of Port Wentworth has held an annual Collard Green Festival each March. The event offers pick-your-own collards for $5 a large bunch, collards and BBQ cooking contests, and multiple vendors. A 1992 study by Richard Westmacott of African American gardens and yards across the state found that, of the Georgia gardeners sampled, 71 percent grew collards, while only 12 percent grew turnip greens.[6]

Further evidence of the strength of collards in Georgia is seen in the state data for sales of collard seedlings by Bonnie Plants, the nation's largest seedling supplier (see table 10). Seedlings are more expensive than seeds and may be purchased more often in places of higher average income. Another factor influencing these sales may be the proximity for Bonnie Plants headquarters in neighboring Alabama for a century. The much lower figures for Louisiana, Arkansas, and Tennessee, and the fairly low numbers for Mississippi make sense, according to all our surveys. Despite the mitigating factors, this data confirms that Georgia is in the collard core.

SOUTH CAROLINA

Ninety-five percent of the South Carolina produce managers interviewed said their top-selling leafy green is collards (our sample included sixty, at least one in every county). In Bamberg, the produce manager at Piggly Wiggly told us that collards are very popular; he sells only small quantities of mustard greens and even fewer turnip greens. He buys greens locally during the fall and winter, really pleasing his favorite customers.

In Andrews, South Carolina, a small town north and inland from Charleston, the produce manager at another Piggly Wiggly store said 75 to 80 percent of the greens he sells are collards. He said Piggly Wiggly has

TABLE 10. 2010–2011 SALES OF COLLARD SEEDLINGS BY STATE OF THE NATION'S LARGEST SUPPLIER, BONNIE PLANTS

State	Total Plants Sold
Georgia	1,181,400
Alabama	966,600
Virginia	785,400
South Carolina	735,000
Florida	702,900
North Carolina	598,500
Mississippi	342,750
Tennessee	44,000
Arkansas	42,000
Louisiana	19,200
Total	5,417,750

Source: Lange, S. 2011. "Collard Plant Sales Data," Personal communication with Edward Davis, July 1.

an advantage over some larger supermarkets in its freedom to buy collards locally, which he does for all the holiday seasons when demand is highest. From these various managers, we learned that in South Carolina—as in parts of Alabama, Florida, and Georgia—people were rather picky about their collards: they would not buy grocery store collards unless they looked fresh and undamaged.

Near a small collard patch in an old city neighborhood of Columbia, South Carolina, under some large pecan trees, sat an elderly man with his eyes closed and face uplifted, clearly enjoying the unseasonal warmth of a January afternoon. This was Elbert Metze, born in 1920 in Little Mountain in the hills northwest of Columbia, population currently 255. "We grew up working a big garden, and cabbage was the main crop." He told us his great-grandfather was a German immigrant. "We made sauerkraut as a neighborhood project, using a huge wooden barrel," he recalled. "Later on, we started making sauerkraut using collards. It was very good. I got my seed from my father. It's a heading collard, milder than the Georgia. The best way is to start the seed in Dixie cups, and then when August comes you want them ready to put out in the garden. When you cook them, my mother always said, roll them up and cut the leaves twice so you don't think you're eating green spaghetti!"

Fresh-picked collards are sold regularly through the fall on Columbia's north side in the parking lot of Ebenezer Lutheran Church. Abraham McFadden drives in on Thursdays to use this free space. He raises a whole range of vegetables through the year and sells them here, but the cost of gasoline has cut into his profits in recent years.

Another indicator of the heart of collard culture comes from survey data produced between 1965 and 1970 for the *Dictionary of Regional American English*. The survey asked such questions as "What kind of vegetables do you eat around here?" The state with the most people answering collards was South Carolina.[7] South Carolina is also the only state where collards are the state vegetable, a result of a 2011 resolution passed by the South Carolina state legislature and signed by the governor. Of course, very few states have a state vegetable, and some people criticized the legislature for spending time on such a trivial matter. One senator who questioned the choice of collards suggested green beans would have been just as appropriate. In response, the governor commended the nine-year-old girl who had proposed collards. She had come up with the idea after a visit to the statehouse where students were encouraged to become active citizens.[8]

South Carolina seems to have more home gardens than most of the other states we visited. Its long settlement history may be one reason for this fact. Most of the state was occupied by the end of the American Revolution, and by 1800 farms were found in all but a few swampy or hilly lands. Cotton plantations wore out soils, but small farms became permanently planted, forests were cleared, and so large gardens were cultivated in a high density decades before they were in some other parts of the South. We suspect that the South Carolina foodways prevalent about 1800 or 1810 had a better chance of survival than those in the "Old Southwest" (the early name for Georgia, Alabama, and Mississippi), partly because during those formative years the latter region was undergoing frontier conflicts with Native Americans, and most farms there were still being chopped out of the forest. South Carolina settlement history is not simple, but it did come earlier, as did the settlement of the coastal plain in North Carolina and Virginia.

Consider, for example, Richlands County, in the center of the state, which by 1800 already had 6,000 residents. Almost no counties west and south of there in Georgia and elsewhere had such numbers, until you reach Louisiana. The cultural traditions in such settled places are older and more established by two or more generations. This area was no longer a frontier. Gardens would have been nearly ubiquitous, for those with the freedom to have one.

Slaves constituted over half of Richland County residents in 1800, so the strength of the African American element must be considered. This exploited culture, constrained and distorted as it was by slavery, must have still had a substantial influence. As geographer Judith Carney has shown, the Low Country's rice plantations were successful because of Africans' knowledge and skills. Slaves were given and sometimes took opportunities, under the overseers' watchful eyes, to "make the land productive."[9]

Cultivating a garden was just one of those opportunities, and although few precise records of what or how garden crops were grown by slaves, they did what they could to thrive in spite of the system. Here is a diary entry

from 1860 by a "plantation mistress" of Richland County, Keziah Goodwyn
Hopkins Brevard:

> October 19, 1860. This is Friday—a boisterous morn this is—I
> shall not look for Mrs. R. today unless there is a great change before 10
> O'clock. Negroes such trying creatures you are—The first thing I saw
> like work this morning was Rosanna with a box of collards out of my
> garden—I have very few there, the hot summer prevented my saving but
> a very few. I have plenty of turnips, gave them as many as they wanted
> yesterday and the day before and intended they should have more when
> they wished. I make John stay in the kitchen in wet weather and try to
> keep her (Rosanna) out of the rain—but she could leave my breakfast
> and go through the rain to deceive me. Oh I wish I had been born in
> a Christian land and never seen or known of slaves of any colour. A
> degraded population is a curse to a country.[10]

Complaining about the behavior of her slaves, Hopkins seems not only re-
sentful toward them and slavery itself, but also simply out of control. She
says the collards come "out of my garden," but her ownership does not prevent the slaves from acting on their own accord. What does this negotiation
over the garden between slaves and masters mean for the history of Southern gardening?

Reanell Bradley, an 80-year-old woman who always has a garden, usually plants two and a half rows of collards and one and a half rows of cabbage.
She lives east of Columbia, on the edge of the coastal plain in the unincor-
porated Wisacky community of Lee County. She likes Green Glaze collards
but didn't grow any of those seed this year. She cooks collards once a week
and cabbage twice a week. In addition to providing vegetables for her family,
Bradley uses her garden to provide for several widow friends in the community, especially in her church, and she says, "every Sunday I make dinner for
my pastor." She gives away a lot of her collards. In addition to collards, she
usually has some turnips and mustard greens in her garden (see fig. 26).

Bradley freezes collards so that she has some for the rest of the year. For freezing, she washes and packs lightly boiled collard leaves in freezer bags. She adds a cup and a half of water to each freezer bag. She says these will keep for several months. Her recipe for collards is included in Chapter Three.

The survey of college students mentioned earlier has an interesting result for South Carolina. As previously explained, the survey was of students in geography and other social science classes at two- and four-year colleges and universities in all ten states of our study area. We asked the question "what kind of greens do you prefer?" Map 5 shows our results, organized by state.

Notice that South Carolina had the strongest showing for collards at 82 percent. That is, of all students from South Carolina giving us a preference, 82 percent said it was for collards. Florida and North Carolina were close behind, tied at 77 percent, and Georgia data showed collards to be nearly as popular there, at 72 percent. For the South as a whole, according to our data, college students prefer collards over other greens. But only 40 percent gave a preference, and although about 10 percent of students told us they eat all the greens and have no preference, our data suggest that more than half of Southern college students don't eat greens.

The mustard greens preference we saw on the landscape in Louisiana (49 percent) and parts of Mississippi is evident in this survey data. A small mustard area we found in Georgia doesn't make much of an impact on the statewide numbers. There is an obvious love of turnip greens (and probably turnips, too) in Arkansas, Tennessee, and Alabama. The important pattern for the collard core is this: the four strongest "collard states" were the Carolinas, Georgia, and Florida.

North Carolina

North Carolina in its far western mountains is a terrain broken by valleys and mountain ridges, where every traveler encounters commercial farms and home gardens with corn, hay, tobacco, and vegetables. Cherokee County, in the state's most extreme southwestern corner, held remaining Cherokee families in isolated village clusters as late as the 1940s. That defiance of President Andrew Jackson's removal decree means that, today, a large percentage of people here have some Cherokee ancestry. This fact relates to our collard story.

Commercial gardens and home vegetable patches in this area tend to favor collards, whereas gardens in the surrounding mountains and counties tend to favor turnip greens instead. There must be a cultural or historical explanation for this situation. Cherokee researchers in the late 1970s noted a local preference for collards.[11] Older folks in this part of Western North Carolina, including also Swain and Jackson counties, relate that collards have long been grown by Cherokee families. One report came from the now retired agricultural extension agent for the Cherokee Reservation, who recalled seeing quite a few collard patches on the reservation.

John Lloyd Smith is a 71-year-old member of the Cherokee tribal community who lives alone on his 15 acres of mostly wooded land. He grows feed corn and hay for a few cattle, but he says, "I spend more of my time in the gardens. That's my home." It's actually two gardens, which total about an acre. The smaller of the two is a sweet potato patch on the lower end, down along the creek. The larger one, on a gentle slope above his house, is a mix of many vegetables, depending on the season. In the fall and winter he grows several rows each of cabbage and collards. Smith eats most of what he grows, freezing some, but gives a lot of produce to neighbors. He informed us that "there is a row of houses up the hill from here that's just widows now, so I take them vegetables when I can."

The current agricultural extension agent, who is also Cherokee, is working to support some seed saving among the community's gardeners. She says local gardeners are used to saving beans that they consider the best, and one gardener saves maize, but she knew of none saving collard seed anymore.

The Cherokee are among the earliest people in America for whom there is a documented record of growing collards. Benjamin Hawkins, while scouting western North Carolina in 1796, came to what is now Swain County, just a few miles from where John Lloyd Smith currently lives, and boldly rode his horse right into a Cherokee village. There were no men there, he reported, and the women communicated to him that the men were out hunting far away while they stayed home and tended the gardens, which included traditional Cherokee crops (corn, beans, and pumpkins), but there were also some European imports: onions, watermelons, and collards.[12] This was a time when almost no whites were settled in the area. The very rapid adoption of European and African plants seems striking.

If collards were grown long ago in Cherokee gardens, how did they get there, well before the Euro-American invasion of Appalachia? Cherokee historians say trade with Europeans was established in the mid-1700s along paths that linked them to Charleston on the coast. Early adoption of the peach and the watermelon from those colonists has been documented and studied by others.[13] Apparently, the Cherokee also adopted the collard. The Cherokee also took up the ownership of African slaves. By 1800, quite a number of Cherokee families were reported to be slave-holders. Could there be a connection between the owning of African slaves and collard adoption? We are still looking for documentation to help us answer this question.

North Carolina's Piedmont region is a place one sees a lot of collard patches. On a 2.5-hour "loop" field trip and count taken in December 2000, ninety-five percent of the gardens contained collards; the remainder of the gardens had turnips. Most patches had fifteen to twenty plants, but some were as large as half an acre, many located near the kitchen door and clearly pampered. In seventy miles, there were twelve collard patches, with almost no other greens. The overall conclusion is that the Piedmont region of Anson, Montgomery, Stanly, and Richmond counties is "collard country."

The coastal plain of North Carolina, which begins around Anson and Richmond counties, is collard core: 95 percent of produce managers said collards are by far their number one selling green; 93 percent of fall/winter gardens grow collards and no other greens. In addition, this is the only region where people argued over the best kind of collard as well as where racial overtones attached to the vegetable were nonexistent.

To find a collard food tradition of the "Old South," look to counties east of the Piedmont, such as Beaufort County. Facing the Pamlico Sound, protected from the ocean by the Outer Banks, and shielded from the urban world by a general lack of four-lane highways and a population of less than 45,000, Beaufort is one of the most collard-oriented counties in the South. First, collard gardens are ubiquitous. Second, the Agricultural Census for 2007 showed eight commercial collard growers in Beaufort County, with an average size of just two acres. No other North Carolina county had that many small commercial growers, very likely dependent on and responding to local demand. Third, our survey of college students indicates this county is collard biased.

Eastern North Carolina may have also been the point of origin for the folk tradition of eating collards on New Year's Eve or New Year's Day. An early record of this tradition from 1933 emanates from the small fishing village of Rodanthe on North Carolina's Outer Banks. A journalist from northern Virginia visited the area during the Great Depression and wrote that during the Christmas season the local folks held their biggest feast not on December 25th but on January 5th or "Twelfth Night," a tradition practiced in many places in Europe. He then added that the feast included wild fowl and collards.[14] This area is one place where modern ideas were uncommon in 1933. Before tourists and retirees reached the Banks in the 1950s, this area was said to be one of the South's more isolated remnant cultures, and perhaps some of the oldest collard traditions were being followed then.

VIRGINIA

Virginia's far southeastern region, called the Tidewater, is part of the collard core, even though home gardens are less common here than on the coastal plain of the Carolinas and Georgia. In spite of this scarcity, historical records confirm that collards were once more common on the land here:

1795: Thomas Jefferson mentions planting collards in his garden at
Monticello.[15] 1824: Farmer John Walker mentions in his diary that
he planted collards.[16]

1829: A doctor in Virginia wrote: "a dyspeptic Irishman can digest a
potato which would kill a Scotchman. So bacon and long collards
might lie easy in the bag of a Virginian, when they would raise a
tempest in that of a New-Englander."[17]

1860s: Civil War soldiers record collards in seven locations in central
and eastern Virginia.

1880: Norfolk area truck farms were growing collards, kale and
cabbage.

1920s: An African American folklorist in Southeast Virginia recorded
this belief: "If collards go to seed the year you plant them, it is a
sign of death in your family."[18]

Still, collards are not mentioned in some other important historic
sources on Virginia. For example, a German traveler in 1784 wrote that
"the pleasure of a fine garden is as yet scarcely known in Virginia. . . . a
few of the most considerable families have made attempts, but commonly
the people are satisfied with planting cabbage and turnips in an enclosed
space, which goes by the name of a garden, and sticking among them a
few uncomely flowers."[19] This traveler's focus was on ornamental gardens,
like the English garden, so perhaps he may not be a reliable narrator. We
have evidence from the Civil War that at least some Virginians had a fondness for collards. Private David Holt of Mississippi marched over much of
that section of Virginia and made this observation of the slave cabins: "Each
house had a vegetable garden and a chicken yard and the slaves were encouraged to supplement the rations they drew with what they raised . . . The
chief vegetable raised in the quarters was collards. The lower leaves were
eaten for greens."[20] His last sentence about the lower leaves is especially significant, given that this cropping habit has been seen in many places now.
The cabbage (heading) collard may not handle this form of harvest so well,

but many types of collard will grow a strong enough stalk to support a plant four feet high, even higher in the mildest climates.

Explaining the Collard Core

So, do most Southerners love collards? Is the South's garden landscape consistent? Foodways and garden landscapes have a complex relationship that makes a broad regional map of the collard "belt" problematic. Recall the earlier mention of Alex Albright's notion, in the *Encyclopedia of Southern Culture*, that collards "delineate a culinary Mason-Dixon line." Our research doesn't confirm that sharp line but a patchwork of collard loyalty (see map 6). In the heart of the Carolina Coastal Plain—and also in parts of Virginia, Alabama, and Georgia—our comprehensive evidence indicates that the majority of people, regardless of age, skin color, or income, favor collards over other greens.

So to the question, "Why are collards particularly popular in the Lowland region of the Carolinas and Georgia and the Alabama Black Belt, but less so elsewhere in the South?" We believe five factors may explain the pattern.

First, the hot climate of these areas does not favor cabbage, which otherwise might have been adopted widely here during the colonial period since it was both popular and more easily stored and transported. Many colonists attempted to grow cabbages, but the heat and the insects were generally too much for them. These problems have been solved in much of the South by the use of more advanced techniques, precise irrigation, and new heat-tolerant varieties. But rural collard traditions were in place by the time these phenomena had become realities.

Second, the soils in much of the Southeastern Coastal Plain are sandy and well drained, which is considered favorable for raising collards. It is partly for this reason that the Sand Hills region on the inner coastal plain of the Carolinas has many commercial collard growers, including W. P. Rawl and Sons. Another crop competitor on the coastal plain has been cotton, but it does better on alluvial soils (those along rivers, such as the Mississippi). To some extent, then, some places where collards were planted had little value for other cash crops. Space may have been made for collards in the Southeast's "waste places."

Third, the small farms common to the Atlantic Coastal Plain in these four states may have preserved traditional rural garden culture more than was possible in some other areas of the South. In particular, eastern North Carolina has many small farms that survived the twentieth century by growing tobacco.[21] Areas dominated by larger plantations may have provided less rural cultural stability, or at least at a much lower density, since sharecroppers often had less landscape influence than small-holders.

Fourth, migrations from the Atlantic Coastal Plain to the interior areas of the South could help explain those pocket areas where collards are preferred. For example, the Gulf Coast, except for Southern Louisiana, was settled mostly by people from the Charleston region. The Upland South was settled, to a significant degree, by migrants from the Mid-Atlantic region, especially Pennsylvania. The migrants came south through the Valley of Virginia and into Tennessee and Kentucky. There are many complexities ignored by this broad stroke, but numerous geographers have preceded us in these conclusions.[22] Our work is simply the first to consider those settlement patterns in a region-wide analysis of collard foodways.

The fifth factor is one we came to recognize only after accounting for all the above. Consider map 6 again and you may see at least four problem areas:

1. Residents of Georgia's Piedmont have a strong collard preference, even though the favorable factors above do not seem to apply there.

2. The mustard anomaly in southeastern Georgia is not explained by any of the four factors. Its history and soils would seem to make it like the areas around it where collards are more popular.

3. The Black Belt, stretching across central Alabama, is a strong collard subregion far outside our main core. Its black soils are different from the sandy soils on the Atlantic Coastal Plain. Its climate is

not significantly different from that found just north or south of it. The large plantation legacy makes this area more parallel to other parts of the Deep South, such as the Mississippi delta.

4. The Cherokee subarea, where we found a strong collard heritage, is surrounded by largely turnip-favoring communities.

The final critical factor seems to be the presence of significant slave populations in the early nineteenth century. Consider the slave population in 1860, shown in map 7. These slave populations were found in three of the four areas just identified, and the mustard area of southeastern Georgia is seen here to have had far fewer slaves. Note the large slave presence in central and western Tennessee in 1860. The lack of significant collard culture there may seem a bit surprising. One possible explanation is that most black people migrated out of this area in the decades after slavery ended. The cultural exchanges there between black and white folk may have been more limited than in much of the Lowland South. The same might be said of parts of the Mississippi delta region. With these exceptions, the areas where slavery was dominant match the areas of a stronger collard preference today.

African Americans were likely the leading preservers of collard culture in the nineteenth century. Even if Europeans introduced collards and carried them into the frontier, African Americans knew their value and appreciated their taste, and so took the lead in preserving the tradition in much of the South. We can assume that whites with less of a leafy greens heritage picked it up by long association with black people. African Americans were often cooking for whites, for years as their slaves and afterwards as servants and maids and restaurant cooks. In many parts of the South, black cooking is highly integrated into dominant white culture—always as a kind of negotiation. The following story by this book's coauthor, Edward H. Davis, about his parents, Lucy and Whitaker, is a case study of such negotiation:

> My mother was raised in Florida and Georgia, but has never liked greens, particularly because of the cooking smell. This may be due to her patrician upbringing. My father was raised a "back-country" Baptist in

the mountains of North Carolina, and likes any vegetable but Brussels sprouts. He had learned to like turnip greens as a child, but after tying the knot he did without some foods, like a good husband ought. Marriage *is* compromise, after all.

The two of them settled and raised me and my brother and my sister in Wadesboro (Anson County), North Carolina, in the southern piedmont, collard country. Mama laughs when she tells the story of how one day when she was away, a neighbor gave my father a bunch of collards. Knowing Mama would be gone for a week, he asked Edna Mae Dean, the unflappable African American woman and excellent cook who served as our maid, and helped raise me, if she would cook the collards. Edna Mae knew that he loved her cooking, so she agreed. A week later, Mama walked into the house and yelled, 'Somebody's been cooking collards!' Usually my mother finishes this story at that point, but the rest of the story is important: Edna Mae and my mother laughed many times about it. But Edna Mae did not cook collards again. My mother had her way. Or did she? Neighbors continued to bring collards to my father— already cooked. And as an adult, I came to love collards and I have cooked them in Mama's kitchen, and she doesn't complain—not much. Somewhere in heaven Edna Mae is laughing.

The pleasures of eating hearty greens and raising a garden are beyond words, of course, and we have not the words even to try. But we do know that even when people suffer terrible abuse, they can find the strength to appreciate the few joys they are allowed to have. Historian Charles Joyner wrote forty years ago about the link between slavery and "soul food," saying, "those [Works Progress Administration] informants who describe the harshest experiences under slavery have very little to say about their food. But . . . whenever a former slave does speak of good times in slavery days, hardly ever does he leave food out of the picture."[23]

In a very real sense, collards are an African American legacy for all Southerners. Whether they become more of a symbol of that heritage, their blend of European and African foodways could make them far more than a side dish and more of a feature. As our work shows, collards were apparently crossing the color line, at least in the collard core of the South, even before Abraham Lincoln was born.

COLLARDS AS AN AFRICAN AMERICAN LEGACY

Southern collards owe a great deal to the people of the African continent. First, they are dark leafy greens, and dark leafy greens were central to African and not European foodways. Europeans boiled cabbage more than collards, and gained less nutrition as a result. Europeans generally ate fewer green vegetables, while Africans put dozens of different leafy greens into many dishes. Even today, the consumption of dark leafy greens is higher among Africans and African Americans than among people of European descent.

Second, the one-pot stews so common in the South probably derive from West African know-how. Ordinary Europeans also ate stews of vegetables and meat, but with generally fewer ingredients than Africans, who regularly included more grains.

Third, pot liquor is more African than European. Europeans had a habit of using pot liquor—and the term is a British one—but Africans seem to have valued it more, for they made it more central to their diets. Southerners who dowse their cornbread in pot liquor are following a habit likely brought from Africa.[24]

Fourth, Africans are responsible for the use of hot peppers either in cooking collards or in flavoring them once on the plate.[25] Europeans, especially the British, had little or no fondness for hot peppers until after centuries of colonialism.

These African foodways are not generally identified by Southerners, and even African Americans seldom hear about this aspect of their heritage. In the final analysis, though, African Americans have retained a certain cultural integrity reflected in their foodways and now shared with other southerners.[26]

Conclusion

This book has explored the cultural and historical geography of an important regional food and food crop. We hope this will be a worthwhile addition to the growing body of geographic scholarship on food.[1] We have sought to accomplish several goals: to describe the traditions of growing the crop and cooking and eating collard greens; to delineate the geography of commercial production; to determine the origin and diffusion of collards to the South from the Old World; to clarify the iconic status of collards in popular culture; and to describe and assess the changing status of collards in the region, as both a landscape feature and a foodway.

The chief joys of our expeditions were the wonderful moments of generosity that collard questions seemed to initiate: "Honey, just come on in and try some of these greens here"; "I'll get you some of our seeds, but you better first have some of my fruitcake"; "I guess I've got time enough between now and the Second Coming. Sit, and let me tell how to cook some *good* collards." All around the South, we were rejuvenated from our road weariness by people who answered a knock on their door, listened to our query about their collard patch, and after the briefest of doubtful pauses, smiled at the chance to tell a story. Some folks were skeptical about the usefulness of food research, as well they should be; but once they realized we shared the same interest in good eating, they opened up. Talking face-to-face about gardens and food seems to make us all more comfortable. If we're ever going to reach our maximum humanity, perhaps it will be through the simple sharing of food.

As we hope is now evident, collards carry more significance than many other foods. First, the nutritionist's case: They hold more nutrients than most other leafy green vegetables, indeed most other foods of any kind; they reduce our risk of a variety of diseases; and they can produce a steady supply of nutritious food during months when other plants fail.

Second, the historian's case: They are one of the world's oldest food plants, ancestral to the more popular broccoli, even to the ancient and now worldly cabbage. Collards cooked with some low-on-the-hog meat provided essential sustenance to generations of Europeans and later to generations of Southerners, whether they were enslaved or free. Collards provide one of the most flavorful reminders of our roots to the land.

Third, the geographer's case: Collards are better matched to the fall and winter seasons of the Lowland South than most food plants and have, therefore, found a niche here while the rest of the world has abandoned them. While less popular in certain parts of the South, collards are perhaps more widely popular among Southerners than any other truly regional food. Grits and sweet tea are other viable contenders, but honestly, can such lightweight foods stand up to the pure guttural power of collard greens?

Finally, the case for cultural meanings: Collards are usually enjoyed after much practice, and their strong smell and somewhat bitter flavor make them a challenge for the novice in search of a new food pleasure. Wherever collards have become established, however, there is clear commitment from the greens' fans. In some places—such as Alligator, Mississippi; Evergreen, Alabama; and Wisacky, South Carolina—collards are localized treasure, a geographic jewel not apparent to the casual tourist, the transient consumer. They may be pegged for profitable use as an exotic commodity and mixed with high-toned ingredients to entice the gourmand and the gullible, but that attraction will soon fade like any fashion. Real, ordinary food such as collard greens may persist in the Southern landscape and in Southern kitchens under the radar of our country's fickle pop culture. Meanwhile, collard commerce, both large- and small-scale, provides a significant income to truck farms.

Some have argued that the South is indelibly marked as different, not just by its history of slavery, the Civil War and Reconstruction, but by a larger geopolitical perspective. If this hypothesis is true, it may be that rural traditions such as the collard patch have little hope for survival. The expansion of the consumer economy will gradually eliminate household-level food production. Through economic globalization, people are discouraged to retain their food independence and encouraged to buy their food, which is increasingly imported. Will that general trend toward globalized and lowest-common-denominator foodways replace regional uniqueness? We hope not!

So what is the significance of collards? In national popular culture, collards are sometimes a soul food, sometimes a badge of rurality proudly worn, and sometimes a mark of poverty. They are also an indelible symbol of the South. Advertisements for a 2005 special issue of *Southern Living* called *Best Kept Secrets of the South's Best Cooks* featured a photo of a plate crowded with five foods: fried chicken, cornbread, black-eyed peas, tomatoes, and collards.[2]

Collards are also, by their obscurity at the national scale, useful as an exotic food. Geographer Wilbur Zelinsky wrote, "Food has become the most accessible—and tempting—entrees into alien cultures."[3] So some ambitious non-Southern chefs seeking a fresh "new" ingredient have taken up collards as though they were unearthing Cleopatra's crown jewels. There is a constant demand for foods previously unknown except to "remote villagers." The collard-and-goat cheese canapés we ate at a recent party were very tasty, but the distinctive collard flavor was not quite detectable.

Another form of collard exoticism is seen in visitors to the South eating any sort of collard concoction in order to experience the South. Food tourism is a booming industry, which depends on a region being a "place of difference." If you are one of the millions of non-Southerners who subscribe to

Southern Living, who could blame you for wanting to find a place that serves "authentic" or "traditional" collards?

After all is said and done, collards are a subject of substantial complexity. The thousands of people we met and heard about and surveyed have not simply chosen to include collards in their yards and in their meals; they have made collards an unspoken link through time. We do that with foods we love. By lifting a plant from the garden today, by chopping its leaves, by cleaning and cooking them, by spicing them just so, we reproduce our past histories and places all at once. In our collards today there lingers the unheralded gardening genius of Britain and Portugal, of the unnamed cooking geniuses of West Africa, of our grandparents and their neighbors; in our collards today is the dedication of commercial farmers and Mexican farm workers, produce managers, and restaurant cooks. All the many hands that brought us these collards tell us who we are and where we are.

Notes

PREFACE

1. African botanists and nutritionists today mourn the rise of European food preferences among urbanized Africans, which is decreasing the role of dark leafy greens in their diets. Ikpe, E. B. (1994). *Food and society in Nigeria: A history of food customs, food economy and cultural change 1900–1989*. Stuttgart: Franz Steiner Verlag.

2. Edge, J. T. (1999). *A gracious plenty: Recipes and recollections from the American South*. New York: G.P. Putnam's Sons.

3. Albright, A. (2007). Collard greens. In Edge, J. T. (Ed.). *The new encyclopedia of Southern culture, V. 7: Foodways*. Chapel Hill: University of North Carolina Press, 172–173.

CHAPTER 1

1. *Record of the Alabama Legislature for 1998*. Retrieved 07–28–2004 from: http://www.legislature.state.al.us/Searchableinstruments/1998%20Regular%20Session/Resolutions/HR294.htm.

2. Lake, P. (2006). Interview by E. H. Davis.

3. Faulkner, W. (1948). *Intruder in the dust*. New York: Random House, 12.

4. Tyson, T. B. (2003). *Blood done sign my name*. New York: Three Rivers Press, 321.

5. Percy, W. (1983). The last Donahue Show. In *Lost in the cosmos: The last self-help book*. New York: Farrar, Straus, and Giroux.

6. Edgerton, C. (2003). *Lunch at the Piccadilly*. Chapel Hill, NC: Algonquin Books, 201–202.

7. Mitchell, M. (1961). *Gone with the wind*. New York: Macmillan, 395. (Original work published 1936).

8. Eady, C. (1999). Florida (poem). *Callaloo* 22(4), 1013.

9. Riley, A. (2005, November). Tablet (poem). *Poetry* 187(2), 92.

10. Chappell, F. (1984). The Monk is deep (poem). In Albright, A. & Whisnant, L. (Eds.). *Leaves of Green: The Collard Poems*. Ayden, NC: Ayden Collard Festival, 75.

11. Smith, W. (1988). Rabbit under a collard leaf (lyrics). *Devil's Box*, 22(3), 39.

Retrieved 08–30–2006 from http://www.ibiblio.org/fiddlers/RAA_RAJ.htm.

12. Wright, M. H. (1999). *Sounds like home: Growing up black and deaf in the South*. Washington, DC: Gallaudet University Press, 22.

13. Butler, E. (1966, February). In tune with the South. *Southern Living* 1(1), 4.

14. Lauder, T. (2007). The *Southern Living* solution: How the *Progressive Farmer* launched a magazine and a legacy. *The Alabama review: A quarterly journal of Alabama history*, 60(3), 186–221.

15. Sturges, L. (1971, January). Southern soul food goes gourmet. *Southern Living*, 6(1), 45.

16. Malveaux, S., Hayes, S., Chetry, K., Hornick, E., Brittain, B., and Cohen, T. (2009, November 25). Obama's first state dinner blends pageantry with politics. CNN Online. Retrieved 07–11–2014 from http://www.cnn.com/2009/POLITICS/11/24/obama.state.dinner/index.html?eref=onion.

17. Columbus Collard Green Festival website, Retrieved 04–28–2011 from http://www.lsba.biz/new.html.

18. Walker, A. (1985, January). On excellence. *Ms. Magazine*, 13, 53.

19. Naylor, G. (1985). *Linden hills*. New York: Penguin.

20. Glave, D. D. (2003). 'A garden so brilliant with colors, so original in its design': Rural African American women, gardening, progressive reform, and the foundation of an African American environmental perspective. *Environmental History* 8(3), 395–411.

21. Stewart, M. A. (1996). *'What nature suffers to groe': Life, labor, and landscape on the Georgia coast, 1680–1920*. Athens: University of Georgia Press.

22. Hatley, T. (1984). Tending our gardens. *Southern Changes*, 6(5), 18–24.

23. Zafar, R. (1999). The signifying dish: Autobiography and history in two black women's cookbooks. *Feminist Studies*, 25(2), 449–469.

24. Harris, J. B. (1989). *Iron pots and wooden spoons*. New York: Atheneum; Mitchell, P. B. (1993). *Soul on rice: African influences on American cooking*. Chatham, VA: Foodways Publications.

25. LATIBAH collard greens museum website, Retrieved 01–29–2011 from http://www.latibahmuseum.org/index.htm.

26. Manshack, C. (2007). Interview in Charlotte, NC, by Edward Davis.

27. Sandomir, R. (1997, April 24). Zoeller learns race remarks carry a price. *New York Times*.

28. Meyer, J. P. (2010, January 15). DPS menu for MLK birthday hard for some to digest. *The Denver Post*. Retrieved 01–20–2011 from http://www.denverpost.com/ci_14176531.

29. MacIntosh, J. & Carrega, C. (2010, February 5). NBC's lost 'soul': 'Racial' menu nixed. *New York Post*. Retrieved 11-20-2010 from http://www.nypost.com/p/news/local/manhattan/nbc_lost_soul_UM3zLzo5eb8QDjm6JsbNwK.

30. Turner, P. A. (1999). Watermelons. In Wilson, D. S. & Gillespie, A. K. (Eds.). *Rooted in America: Foodlore of popular fruits and vegetables*. Knoxville: University of Tennessee, 211–223.

31. Fager, C. (2000, February). Dr. King's dinner. *American Heritage* 51(1), 28.

32. Wright, R. (1945). *Black boy: A record of childhood and youth*. New York: Harper & Bros., 114, 152, 158, 284.

33. Bone, R. (1974). Richard Wright. *American writers, Vol. 4*. New York: Charles Scribner's Sons, 474–497.

34. Larkin, C. (2006). On being poor. In Chuck Larkin, Storyteller. Retrieved 07-01-2006 from http://chucklarkin.com/stories.html.

35. Griggs, J. M. (1898). Speech before the House of Representatives, *Congressional Record*, March 15, 2830–2832.

36. Twain, M. (1982). *Puddn'head Wilson, A tale*. Reprinted in M. Twain. *Mississippi writings*. New York: Library of America. (Original work published 1894.)

37. O'Connor, F. (1955). A stroke of good fortune. In *A good man is hard to find and other stories*. San Diego, CA: Harcourt Brace Jovanovich.

38. Sollein, S. (2005). Interview with E. H. Davis.

Chapter 2

1. Elfer, M. (1940). *Opie Read*. Detroit: Boyten Miller Press.

2. Lewis, H. C. (1969). *Odd leaves from the life of a Louisiana swamp doctor*. Upper Saddle River, NJ: Literature House, 152–153. (Original work published 1850.) Retrieved 06-11-2004 from http://docsouth.unc.edu/southlit/lewis/lewis.xml.

3. Hilliard, S. (1969). Hog meat and cornpone: Food habits in the ante-bellum South. *Proceedings of the American Philosophical Society* 113(1), 1–13.

4. Davis, W. C. (2003). *A taste for war: The culinary history of the blue and the gray*. Mechanicsburg, PA: Stackpole Books.

5. ProChef SmartBrief. (2011). Reader Poll for June 28, Retrieved 06-28-2011 from http://www.smartbrief.com/news/CIA/poll_result.jsp?pollName=C8EB620-B-1A7D-411A-A348-6A67F03906FE&issueid=7136E348-0CE8-4693-B3E0-9CCC4BF917A0.

6. East, C., (Ed.). (1991). *Sarah Morgan: The Civil War diary of a Southern woman.* New York: Touchstone, 54.

7. Carmer, C. (1934). *Stars fell on Alabama.* New York: Doubleday.

8. Kerr, M. L. (1992). Collard greens. *Southern Exposure*, 20, 64.

9. Fielder, H. (1883). *A Sketch of the life and times and speeches of Joseph E. Brown.* Springfield, MA: Press of Springfield Printing Company (electronic version in Digital Library of Georgia), 313.

10. Anon. (1862, August 14). Our hospitals. *Savannah Republican*, 2.

11. Daniel, L. J. (1991). *Soldiering in the Army of Tennessee: A portrait of life in a Confederate army.* Chapel Hill: University of North Carolina Press, 60.

12. Thornburgh, A. (1865). Report on gangrene, C. S. Military Prison Hospital, Andersonville, Ga. *Union and Confederate correspondence, orders, Etc., relating To prisoners of war and state from January 1, 1865, to the End.—#26 O.R., Series II, V. 8[S# 121]* Retrieved 05-20-2007 from http://www.civilwarhome.com/andersonville-gangrene.htm.

13. Gates, P. W. (1965). *Agriculture and the Civil War.* New York: Alfred P. Knopf, 101–102.

14. Sylvest, T. A. (2008). *Collard greens: Growing up on a Sandhill subsistence farm in Louisiana during the Great Depression.* Bloomington, IN: Authorhouse.

15. Lockett, S. (1969). *Louisiana as it is.* L. C. Post. (Ed.). Baton Rouge: Louisiana State University Press, 48. (Original work published 1871.)

16. Cawthon, J. A. (1969). Letters of a north Louisiana private to his wife, 1862–1865. *Historic Claiborne.* Homer, LA: Claiborne Parish Historical Association, 9–21. Retrieved 03-20-2009 from http://files.usgwarchives.net/la/claiborne/history/parish/hc69.txt.

17. Miller, J. C. (1934). *Collards: A truck crop for Louisiana.* Baton Rouge, LA: Louisiana State University.

18. Cheatham, M. L. & Elliott, P. (2006). *The collard patch: The best collard cookbook in the world.* Ruston, LA: Blue Moon Books.

19. Anon. (1996, August 19). In the kitchen with—Elvis? *Newsweek* 128(8), 68.

20. Jonsson, P. (2006, February 6). Backstory: Southern discomfort food. *The Christian Science Monitor*. Retrieved 11-06-2006 from http://www.csmonitor.com/2006/0206/p20s01-lifo.html.

21. Wilson, J. S. (1860). Health Department. *Godey's Lady's Book*, 60, 178.

22. Clifford, A. T. (2010). Effects of common culinary techniques on the antioxidants in collard greens. Masters' thesis, Food, nutrition and culinary science, Clemson University.

23. Bazzano, L. A. 2008. "Effects of Soluble Dietary Fiber on Low-density Lipoprotein Cholesterol and Coronary Heart Disease Risk." *Current Atherosclerosis Reports* 10, 6 (December), 473–477.

24. Heaney, R. P., Davies, K. M., Barger-Lux, M. J. 2002. "Calcium and Weight: Clinical Studies," *Journal of the American College of Nutrition* 21, 2 (April), 152S–155S.

25. Canner, P. L., Berge, K. G., Wenger, N. K. , Stamler, J., Friedman, L., Prineas, R. J., Friedewald, W. 1986. "Fifteen Year Mortality in Coronary Drug Project Patients: Long-term Benefit with Niacin," *Journal of the American College of Cardiology* 8, 6 (December), 1245–1255. http://www.ncbi.nlm.nih.gov/pubmed/3782631.

26. Weimann, B. I., Hermann, D. 1999. "Studies on Wound Healing: Effects of Calcium D-Pantothenate on the Migration, Proliferation and Protein Synthesis of Human Dermal Fibroblasts in Culture," *International Journal of Vitamin and Nutrient Research* 69, 2, 113–119.

27. Li, C., Ford, E. S., Zhao, G., Balluz, L. S., Giles, W. H., and Liu, S. 2010. "Serum Alpha-Carotene Concentrations and Risk of Death among US Adults— The Third National Health and Nutrition Examination Survey Follow-up Study" *Archives of Internal Medicine,* Published online (Nov. 22) doi:10.1001/archinternmed.2010.440.

28. DeLorenze, G. N., McCoy, L., Tsai, A. L., Quesenberry Jr., C. P., Rice, T., Il'yasova, D., and Wrensch, M. 2010. "Daily Intake of Antioxidants in Relation to Survival among Adult Patients Diagnosed with Malignant Glioma," *BioMed Central Cancer* 10:215. doi:10.1186/1471-2407-10-215.

29. Hawkins, B. D. (2005). "Milk matters: African Americans are not getting enough calcium, one of two emerging health issues to be concerned about, researcher says." *Black Issues in Higher Education* 21(25), 30.

30. Tseng, M. & DeVellis, R. F. (2001). "Fundamental dietary patterns and their correlates among U. S. whites." *Journal of the American Dietetic Association* 101(8), 929.

CHAPTER 3

1. Nathan, J. (2003, June 4). HOME COOKING; East Meets South at a Delta Table. *New York Times.* Retrieved 06–26–2014 from http://www.nytimes.com /2003/06/04/dining/home-cooking-east-meets-south-at-a-delta-table.html.

2. Fisher, A. (1995). *What Mrs. Fisher knows about old Southern cooking.* Bedford, MA: Applewood Books. (Original work published 1881)

3. Smith, M. S. (1885). *Virginia Cookery-book.* New York: Harper & Bros., 23.

4. Bower, A. L. (2007). (Ed.). *African American foodways: Explorations of history and culture.* Urbana: University of Illinois.

5. See the admirable David Walker Lupton African American cookbook collection at the University of Alabama. Retrieved 10-04-2005 from http://www.lib. ua.edu/lupton/luptonlist.htm.

6. De Knight, F. (1948). *A date with a dish: A cook book of Negro American recipes.* New York: Heritage.

7. Jeffries, B. (1969). *Soul food cookbook.* Indianapolis: Bobbs-Merrill, 57.

CHAPTER 4

1. Lee, H. (1960). *To kill a mockingbird.* New York: HarperCollins, 7.

2. Louv, R. (2008). *Last child in the woods.* Chapel Hill, NC: Algonquin Books.

3. Carter, J. (2001). *An hour before daylight: Memories of a rural boyhood.* New York: Simon & Schuster, 34.

4. Rowland, W. (1978). Ain't got no screens. In Terrill, T. E. & Hirsch, J. (Eds.). *Such as us: Southern voices of the thirties.* Chapel Hill: University of North Carolina Press, 55.

5. Federal Writers' Project. (1941). Volume II: Arkansas narratives. *Slave narratives: A folk history of slavery in the United States.* Washington, DC: Works Progress Administration, 212.

6. Works Progress Administration. (1941). Early settlers' personal history questionnaire: William Smith. University of Arkansas Libraries Special Collections. Retrieved 01-24-2007 from http://libinfo.uark.edu/SpecialCollections/wpa/smith.pdf.

7. Griessman, B. E. & Henson, C. T. (1975). The history and social topography of an ethnic island in Alabama. *Phylon* 36(2), 97–112.

8. Higgins, A. (2006, September 13). Tending the soul: Boomers fueling surge in vegetable gardening. *Washington Post.*

9. Respondents were asked for their hometown, county, and state, which allowed us to map the data based on where students were from rather than where they were attending college.

10. Blackstone, J. H. & Inman, B. T. (1942). *Food habits of consumer groups in small towns of Alabama, Bulletin No. 252.* Auburn, AL: Alabama Polytechnic Institute.

11. Halbert, H. S. & Ball, T. H. (1895). *The Creek War of 1813 and 1814.* Chicago: Donohue & Henneberry. Retrieved 02-24-2004 from http://homepages.rootsweb.com/~cmamcrk4/hbtoc.html.

12. Anon. (1833, August 24). Letter to the editor. *Farmer's Register,* 249.

13. Quoted on p. 377 in Bonner, J. C. (1945). Plantation architecture of the Lower South on the eve of the Civil War. *The Journal of Southern History,* 11(3), 370–388.

CHAPTER 5

1. Hazzard, T. F. (1831). On vegetable gardens, and the great advantages of a much more general use of vegetable diet. *Southern Agriculturist,* 4(12), 627–631.

2. USDA News Release. (2011, August 5). More than 1,000 new farmers markets recorded across country. Retrieved from http://www.ams.usda.gov/AMSv1.0/farmersmarkets.

3. Kingsolver, B., Hopp, S. J. & Kingsolver, C. (2007). *Animal vegetable miracle: A year of food life.* New York: Harper Perennial.

4. "H-2A Temporary Agricultural Program," United States Department of Labor, Employment & Training Administration. Retrieved 07-1-2014 from http://www.foreignlaborcert.doleta.gov/h-2a.cfm.

5. Kirby, J. T. (1987). *Rural worlds lost: The American South, 1920–1960.* Baton Rouge, LA: Louisiana State University Press.

6. Lucier, G. (1998, January/February). Americans eating more leafy green vegetables. *Agricultural Outlook.* USDA Economic Research Service.

7. Berry, W. (1977). The unsettling of America: Culture and agriculture. New York: Avon.

CHAPTER 6

1. Georgia Genealogical Society. (2005). Libraries in Georgia with genealogical holdings: Roddenberry Memorial Library, Cairo, Georgia. Retrieved 12-05-2005 from http://www.gagensociety.org/pdf_files/libcairo.pdf.

2. Landreth, D. (1844). *Descriptive catalogue of the garden seeds cultivated on the grounds of David Landreth*. Philadelphia: D. Landreth. In National Agricultural Library, Special Collections, 27.

3. Clark, T. D. (1944). *Pills, petticoats, and plows: The Southern country store*. Norman: University of Oklahoma Press, 139.

4. Thomas, J. (1997). *Washington's small-seeded vegetable seed industry*. Washington State Cooperative extension publication EB1829. Pullman, WA: Washington State University.

5. Dillon. M. (2006). A brief history of the development of the seed industry: The shift from public to private seed systems. Retrieved 05-15-2006 from http://www.seedalliance.org/index.php?page=SeminisMonsanto.

6. Olson, S. M. & Freeman, J. H. (2005). Selecting collard varieties based on yield, plant habit and bolting. University of Florida Extension, Bulletin HS 1101. Retrieved 01-05-2008 from http://edis.ifas.ufl.edu/pdffiles/HS/HS35300.pdf.

7. Brookfield, H., Parsons, H., and Brookfield, M. (Eds.). (2003). *Agrodiversity: Learning from farmers across the world*. Tokyo: United Nations University.

8. See the Southern Exposure Seed Exchange, based in Charlottesville, VA; and for modern seed-saving, see Deppe, C. (1993). *Breed your own vegetable varieties*. Boston: Little, Brown & Co.

9. Atwater, W. O. & Woods, C. D. (1897). *Dietary studies with reference to the food of the Negro in Alabama in 1895 and 1896. U. S. D. A. Bulletin Number 38*. Washington, DC: Government Printing Office.

10. Farnham, M. (2011). Personal communication with E. H. Davis (June 30).

CHAPTER 7

1. Greene, W. (2012). *Vegetable gardening the Colonial Williamsburg way: 18th-century methods for today's organic gardener*. Emmaus, PA: Rodale Books.

2. Smith, J. (1631). *The generall historie of Virginia, New-England, and the Summer*

Isles. London: Michael Sparkes, 169. University of North Carolina Electronic Edition of 2006, Retrieved 06-28-2001 from http://docsouth.unc.edu/southlit/smith/smith.html.

3. Snogerup, S. (1980). The wild forms of the *Brassica oleracea* group (2n=18) and their possible relations to the Cultivated Ones. In Tsunda, S. & K. Hinata, K. (Eds). *Brassica crops and wild allies: Biology and breeding* (Tokyo: Japan Scientific Press), 33–49; Gomez-Campo, C., Aguinagalde, I., Ceresuela, J., Lázaro, A., Martínez-Laborde, J., Parra-Quijano, M., Simonetti, E., Torres, E., & Tortosa, M. (2005). An exploration of wild *Brassica oleracea* L. germplasm in northern Spain. *Genetic Resources and Crop Evolution,* 52(1), 7–13.

4. Schery, R. W. (1972). *Food for man.* Englewood Cliffs, NJ: Prentice Hall.

5. Mitchell, N. D. (1976). The status of *Brassica oleracea* L. subsp. *oleracea* (wild cabbage) in the British Isles. *Watsonia* 11, 97–103.

6. Gomez-Campo, C., Aguinagalde, I., Ceresuela, J., Lázaro, A., Martínez-Laborde, J., Parra-Quijano, M., Simonetti, E., Torres, E., & Tortosa, M. (2005). An exploration of wild *Brassica oleracea* L. germplasm in northern Spain. *Genetic resources and crop evolution,* 52(1), 7–13.

7. Sauer, J. (1993). *Historical geography of crop plants: A select roster.* Boca Raton, FL: CRC Press.

8. Bye, R. A. (1981). Quelites: Ethnoecology of edible greens, past, present, future. *Journal of ethnobiology* 1, 109–123.

9. Tsunoda, S. and Gomez-Campo, C. (1980). *Brassica crops and wild allies.* Tokyo: Japan Scientific Societies Press, 110.

10. Zohary, D. & Hopf, M. (1993). *Domestication of plants in the Old World: The origin and spread of cultivated plants in West Asia, Europe, and the Nile Valley, Second Edition* (Oxford: Clarendon); Leach, H. M. (1982). On the origins of kitchen gardening in the Ancient Near East. *Garden History,* 10(1), 1–16.

11. Divaret, I. & Thomas, G. (1998). Use of RAPD markers to analyze the genetic variability of a collection of Brassica oleracea L. In: Thomas, G. & Monteiro, A. A. (Eds.): Proceedings of the International Symposium on Brassicas. *Acta Horticultura,* 459, 255–262.

12. Laghetti, G., Martignano, F., Falco, V., Cifarelli, S., Gladis, T. & Hammer, K. 2005. Mugnoli: a neglected race of *Brassica oleracea* L. from Salento (Italy). *Genetic Resources and Crop Evolution* 52(5), 635–639.

13. Sauer, J. (1993). *Historical geography of crop plants: A select roster.* Boca Raton, FL: CRC Press, 26.

14. Landsberg, S. (1996). *The medieval garden.* London: British Museum Press, 2.

15. Landsberg, S. (1996). *The medieval garden.* London: British Museum Press, 118.

16. Thompson, K. F. (1976). Cabbages, kales (*Brassica oleracea*). In N. W. Simmonds (Ed.). *Evolution of crop plants.* London: Longman, 49–52.

17. Farnham, M. W. & Garrett, J. T. (1996). Importance of collard and kale genotype for winter production in southeastern United States. *HortScience, 31,* 1210–1214.

18. Egerton, J. (1993). *Southern food: At home, on the road, in history* (Chapel Hill: University of North Carolina Press), 13.

19. Gibbon, E. (2003). Central Africa. In S. H. Katz, Ed. *Encyclopedia of food and culture. V. 1.* New York: Charles Scribner's Sons, 25.

20. MacDonald, S. (2003, June 1). In Charleston, menus are food for questions. *The Seattle Times.*

21. Carney, J. A. (2001). *Black rice: The African origins of rice cultivation in the Americas.* Cambridge, MA: Harvard University Press.

22. Hamilton, C. Y. (2001). *Cuisines of Portuguese encounters* (New York: Hippocrene).

23. Wiersema, J. & Leon, B. (1999). *World economic plants: A standard reference* (Boca Raton, FL: CRC Press).

24. On the geography of the slave source regions, see Davidson, B. (1961). *Black mother: The years of the African slave trade.* Boston: Little, Brown & Co.; on the inability of European cool-season vegetables to produce seed in Africa, see Alpern, S. B. (1992). The European introduction of crops into West Africa in precolonial times. *History in Africa,* 19, 13–43.

25. Chweya, J. A. (1985). Identification and nutritional importance of indigenous leaf vegetables in Kenya. *Acta Horticulturae* 153, 99–106; Getahun, A. (1974). The role of wild plants in the native diet of Ethiopia. *Agro-Ecosystems* 1, 45–56; Ikpe, E. B. (1994). *Food and society in Nigeria: A history of food customs, Food economy and cultural change 1900–1989.* Stuttgart: Franz Steiner Verlag; Johnson, E. J. & Johnson, T. J. (1976). Economic plants in a rural Nigerian market. *Economic Botany* 30, 375–381; Martin, F. W. (1984). *CRC Handbook of tropical food crops.* Boca Raton, FL: CRC Press.

26. See for example Caillie, R. (1965). *Journal d'un voyage a Temboctou et a Jenne dans l'Afrique Centrale.* Paris: Editions Anthropos. (Original work published 1830.)

27. Abrahams, R. D. and Szwed, J. F. (Eds.). (1983). *After Africa: Extracts from*

British travel accounts and journals of the seventeenth, eighteenth and nineteenth centuries concerning the slaves, their manners, and customs in the British West Indies. New Haven, CT: Yale University; Burkill, H. M. (1985). *The useful plants of west tropical Africa, Vol. A–D* (2nd ed.). Kew, UK: Royal Botanic Garden; Gelfand, M. (1971). *Diet and tradition in an African culture.* Edinburgh, UK: E & S. Livingstone; Gbile, Z. O. (1983). Indigenous and adapted African vegetables. *Acta Horticulturae,* 123 (Sixth African Horticultural Symposium).

28. Abbiw, D. K. (1990). *Useful plants of Ghana: West African uses of wild and cultivated plants.* Kew, England: Royal Botanic Gardens; Denton, L., Swarup, V. & Nath, P. (1983). Genetic resources of vegetable crops in Nigeria. *Acta Horticulturae,* 123 (Sixth African Horticultural Symposium).

29. Alade, I. (1985). Classification of Nigerian foods: A review. *Food and Nutrition Bulletin 7,* 2, (June); Dalziel, J. M. (1948). *Useful plants of west tropical Africa.* London: Crown agents for the Colonies; Delaney, M. R. (1969). Official report of the Niger Valley exploring party. In Delaney, M. R. & Campbell, R. (Eds.). *Search for a place: Black Africa and separatism, 1860.* Ann Arbor, MI: University of Michigan. (Original work published 1860.)

30. Freidberg, S. (2001). Gardening on the edge: The social conditions of unsustainability on an African urban periphery. *Annals of the Association of American Geographers,* 91(2), 349–369.

31. Steckle, J. (1972). *The effects of industrialization on food consumption patterns: A study of two Ewe villages in Ghana. Technical Publication No. 20.* Legon: University of Ghana.

32. Friedberg, S. (2001) Gardening on the edge: The social conditions of unsustainability on an African urban periphery. *Annals of the Association of American Geographers,* 91(2), 356.

33. Dhewa, C. (2003, September 1). The old ones are the best. *The New Agriculturist.* Retrieved 04–03–2010 from *http://www.new-ag.info/03-5/focuson/focuson5. html*; van Epenhuijsen, C. W. (1974). *Growing native vegetables in Nigeria.* Rome: Food and Agriculture Organization.

34. Huffman, A. (2004). *Mississippi in Africa.* New York: Gotham Books.

35. Kufogbe, S. K. (2005). Interview in the Dept. of Geography, University of Ghana, by E. H. Davis.

36. Markwei, C. (2005). Interview in the Dept. of Botany, University of Ghana, by E. H. Davis.

37. Monteiro , A. A. (2006). Interview in the Instituto Superior de Agronomia, Lisbon, Portugal by E. H. Davis.

38. Hedrick, U. P. (Ed.). (1972). *Sturtevant's edible plants of the world*. New York: Dover.

39. Barrett, O. W. (1925). The food plants of Porto Rico. *Journal of the Department of Agriculture of Porto Rico*, 9(2), 61–208.

40. Thomasson, D. (1994). Montserrat kitchen gardens: Social functions and development potential. *Caribbean Geographer* 5(1), 20–31.

41. Crosby, A. W. (1972). *The Columbian exchange: Biological and cultural consequences of 1492*. Westport, CT: Greenwood, 67.

42. Hedrick, U. P. (Ed.). (1972). *Sturtevant's edible plants of the world*. New York: Dover; Benzoni, G. (2010). *History of the New World: Showing his travels in America from A. D. 1541 to 1546; with some particulars of the island of Canary*. (Smyth, W. H., ed. and trans.). London, Hakluyt Society. (Original work published 1857.)

43. Watts, D. (1987). *The West Indies: Patterns of development, culture and environmental change since 1492*. Cambridge, UK.: Cambridge University Press.

44. Goodwin, G. (1977). *Cherokees in transition: A study of changing culture and environment prior to 1775*. Department of Geography Research Paper 181. Chicago: University of Chicago.

45. Wood, P., Waselkov, G. & Hatley, T. (Eds.). (1989). *Powhatan's mantle: Indians in the colonial Southeast*. Lincoln: University of Nebraska.

46. Katz, W. L. (1986). *Black Indians: A hidden heritage*. New York: Atheneum Books, 22–26.

47. Simpson, J. A. & Weiner, E. S. C. (Eds.). (1989). *The Oxford English Dictionary*. New York: Oxford University.

48. Dickson, R. W. (1807). *Practical Agriculture*. London: Phillips, 71, 85.

49. Anon. (1823, October 2). Advertisement. *The London Times*. Also see Anon. (1834, December 28). Letter. *Bell's Life in London and Sporting Chronicle* (London, England), 640; Anon. (1826, January 22). Letter. *Bell's Life in London and Sporting Chronicle* (London, England), 204, 31.

50. Halliwell-Phillipps, J. O. (1968). *A dictionary of archaic and provincial words, obsolete phrases, proverbs, and ancient customs, from the fourteenth century*. Detroit: Gale Research, 264. (Original work published 1850.)

51. Lowsley, B. (1888). *A glossary of Berkshire words and phrases*. London: English Dialect Society, 64. Retrieved 12–30–2009 from *http://www.archive.org/ stream/aglossaryberkshoolowsgoog/aglossaryberkshoolowsgoog_djvu.txt*; Anon. (1881).

Oxfordshire glossary supplement. Oxford: Phillips.

52. Feltman, W. (1969). *The journal of Lieut. William Feltman*. New York: New York Times. (Original work published 1781–1782.)

53. Hutchins, T. (1968). An account of the Genesee Tract. In Imlay, G. *A topographical description of the western territory of North America*. New York: S. Campbell. (Original work published 1797.)

54. Hawkins, B. (1916). *Letters of Benjamin Hawkins, 1796–1806*, Georgia Historical Society Collections, V. 9. Savannah, GA: Georgia Historical Society.

55. Halbert, H. S. & Ball, T. H. (1895). *The Creek War of 1813 and 1814*. Montgomery, AL: White, Woodruff & Fowler.

56. Singleton, A. (1824). In Knight, H. (Ed.). *Letters from the South and West*. Boston: Richardson and Lord, 106. doi: http://hdl.loc.gov/loc.gdc/lhbtn.21522.

57. Thorburn, G. & Son. (1822). *Catalogue of kitchen garden, herb, flower, tree and grass seeds*. New York: Clayton & Van Norden.

58. An inventory of the property of Barney Ballance, deceased, taken February, 1830. Hyde County, NC, Record of Wills, Book #4, part II.

59. Before 1750, "colewort" usually meant any *Brassica* plant. For example, the following list of garden plants being grown in the Carolina colony in 1682 is very likely lumping all the *Brassicas* under that name: "Potatoes, Lettice, Coleworts, Parsnip, Turnip, carrot, and Reddish . . ." Such confusion of terms renders distinction of the "true" colewort or collard difficult for that earlier time period.

60. Harvey, J. H. (1981). *Medieval gardens*. London: Batsford.

61. Thick, M. (1990). Garden seeds in England before the late eighteenth century: I. Seed growing. *Agricultural History Review*, 38(1), 58–71.

62. Thick, M. (1990). Garden seeds in England before the late eighteenth century: I. Seed growing. *Agricultural History Review*, 38(1), 59.

63. Larkin, J. (1988). *The reshaping of everyday life, 1790–1840*. New York: Harper Perennial.

64. Levenstein, H. A. (1988). *Revolution at the table: The transformation of the American diet*. New York: Oxford University, 3.

65. Leighton, A. (1976). *American gardens in the eighteenth century*. Boston: Houghton Mifflin, 213.

66. Hedrick, U. P. (1950). *A history of horticulture in America to 1860*. New York: Oxford University, 183.

67. e.g., Anon. (1767, March 26). Advertisement. *The Virginia Gazette*, 827, 3,

which advertises seeds for "summer and winter coleworts" and several kinds of cabbage.

68. Farnham, M., Davis, E. H., Morgan, J. T., & Smith. P. (2007). Neglected landraces of collard. *Genetic Resources and Crop Evolution, 52,* 797–801.

69. Gerard, J. (1975). *The herbal, or General history of plants.* New York: Dover. (Original work published 1633.)

70. Gerard, J. (1975). *The herbal, or General history of plants.* New York: Dover. (Original work published 1633), 313.

71. Gerard, J. (1975). *The herbal, or General history of plants.* New York: Dover. (Original work published 1633), 316.

72. Miller, P. (1759). *The gardener's dictionary.* London: C. Rivington.

73. Oldham. C. H. (1948). *Brassica crops and allied cruciferous crops.* London: Crosby Lockwood & Sons, 129.

74. Anon., quoted in Bonham-Carter, V. 1952. *The English village.* Harmondsworth: Penguin, 77–78.

Chapter 8

1. Lewis, E. & Peacock, S. (2003). *The gift of southern cooking.* New York: Alfred Knopf, 156.

2. Scheper-Hughes, N. (2004). Anatomy of a quilt: The Gee's Bend freedom quilting bee. *Southern Cultures* 10(3), 88–98.

3. Anon. (1825, August 20). Market report. *Pensacola Gazette and West Florida Advertiser.*

4. Eady, C. (1999). Florida. *Callaloo* 22(4), 1013.

5. Bouknight, W. R. (1998, April 16). Putting bells in United Methodist steeples. Confessing movement talk. Retrieved from http://www.confessingumc.org/doc_bouknight_bells.html.

6. Westmacott, R. (1992). *African American gardens and yards.* Knoxville, TN: University of Tennessee Press, 185.

7. Cassidy, F. G. (1985). *Dictionary of regional American English, Vol. 1: A–C.* Cambridge, MA: Harvard University Press.

8. Anon. (2011, June 3). It's official: Collards are S.C. state vegetable. *The Post and Courier* (Charleston, SC). Retrieved 06-01-2011 from http://www.postandcourier.com/news/2011/jun/03/its-official-collards-are-sc-state-vegetable/.

9. Carney, J. & Rosomoff, R. (2010). *In the shadow of slavery: Africa's botanical legacy in the Atlantic world.* Berkeley: University of California Press.

10. Moore, J. H., ed. (1993). *A plantation mistress on the eve of the Civil War: The diary of Keziah Goodwyn Hopkins Brevard, 1860–61.* Columbia: University of South Carolina.

11. Terry, R. & Bass, M. (1984). Food practices of families in an eastern Cherokee township. *Ecology of Food and Nutrition,* 14, 63–70.

12. Hawkins, B. (1916). *Letters of Benjamin Hawkins, 1796–1806, Georgia Historical Society Collections, V. 9.* Savannah: Georgia Historical Society.

13. Goodwin, G. (1977). *Cherokees in transition: A study of changing culture and environment prior to 1775.* Department of Geography Research Paper 181. Chicago: University of Chicago.

14. Anon. (1933, January 4). Christmas Eve is observed in Carolina town. *Free-lance Star* (Fredericksburg, VA).

15. Betts, E. M. (Ed.). (1999). *Thomas Jefferson's garden book, 1766–1824.* Charlottesville, VA: Thomas Jefferson Memorial Foundation, 71, 224.

16. Bushman, C. L. (2001). *In old Virginia: Slavery, farming and society in the journal of John Walker.* Baltimore, MD: Johns Hopkins University Press, 24.

17. Hall, M. (1829). An essay on disorders of the digestive organ, and general health and on their complications. *The Southern Review* (Charleston), IV (August), 225.

18. Waters, D. J. (1983). *Strange ways and sweet dreams: Afro-American folklore from the Hampton Institute.* Boston, MA: G. K. Hall, 362.

19. Schoepf, J. D. (1911). *Travels in the Confederation, 1783–1784* (A. J. Morrison, ed. and trans.). Philadelphia: William J. Campbell, 76. (Original work published 1784.)

20. Cockrell, T. D. & Ballard, M. B. (Eds.). (1995). *A Mississippi rebel in the Army of Northern Virginia: The Civil War memoirs of Private David Holt* (Baton Rouge: Louisiana State University), 37–38.

21. Hart, J. F. (1991). *The land that feeds us.* New York: W.W. Norton & Co., 277–290.

22. Meinig, D. W. (1993). *The shaping of America, V.2: Continental America, 1800–1867.* New Haven, CT: Yale University Press, 221–311.

23. Joyner, C. W. (1971). Soul food and the Sambo stereotype: Foodlore from the Slave Narrative Collection. *Keystone Folklore Quarterly,* 16, 171–178.

24. Harris (2005).

25. Shiflet, L. R. (2004). West African food traditions in Virginia foodways. Master's thesis in history, East Tennessee State University.

26. Ferguson, L. (1992). *Uncommon ground: Archaeology and early African America, 1650–1800.* Washington, DC: Smithsonian Institution.

Conclusion

1. Shortridge, B. G. & Shortridge, J. R. (1995). Cultural geography of American foodways: An annotated bibliography. *Journal of Cultural Geography,* 15, 79–108.

2. Southern Living Magazine. (2005). *Best kept secrets of the South's best cooks.* Birmingham, AL: Oxmoor House.

3. Zelinsky, W. (2001). *The enigma of ethnicity: Another American dilemma.* Iowa City: University of Iowa Press, 117.

Additional Reading

Albright, A. (2007). Collard greens. In Edge, J. T. (Ed.). *The new encyclopedia of Southern culture, V. 7: Foodways.* Chapel Hill: University of North Carolina Press, 172–173.

Alpern, S. B. (1992). The European introduction of crops into West Africa in pre-colonial times. *History in Africa,* 19, 13–43.

Bower, A. L. (2007). (Ed.). *African American foodways: Explorations of history and culture.* Urbana: University of Illinois Press.

Carney, J. (2001). *Black rice: The African origins of rice cultivation in the Americas.* Cambridge, MA: Harvard University Press.

Carney, J. & Rosomoff, R. (2010). *In the shadow of slavery: Africa's botanical legacy in the Atlantic world.* Berkeley: University of California Press.

Carter, J. (2001). *An hour before daylight: Memories of a rural boyhood.* New York: Simon & Schuster.

Cheatham, M. L. & Elliott, P. (2006). *The collard patch: The best collard cookbook in the world.* Ruston, LA: Blue Moon Books.

Crosby, A. W. (1972). *The Columbian exchange: Biological and cultural consequences of 1492.* Westport, CT: Greenwood.

Edge, J. T. (1999). *A gracious plenty: Recipes and recollections from the American South.* New York: G.P. Putnam's Sons.

Egerton, J. (1993). *Southern food: At home, on the road, in history.* Chapel Hill: University of North Carolina Press.

Farnham, M. W. & Garrett, J. T. (1996). Importance of collard and kale genotype for winter production in southeastern United States. *HortScience,* 31, 1210–1214.

Farnham, M., Davis, E. H., Morgan, J. T., & Smith. P. (2007). Neglected land races of collard. *Genetic Resources and Crop Evolution,* 52, 797–801.

Ferguson, L. (1992). *Uncommon ground: Archaeology and early African America, 1650–1800.* Washington, DC: Smithsonian Institution.

Freidberg, S. (2001). Gardening on the edge: The social conditions of unsustainability on an African urban periphery. *Annals of the Association of American Geographers,* 91(2), 349–369.

Gbile, Z. O. (1983). Indigenous and adapted African vegetables. *Acta Horticulturae,* 123 (Sixth African Horticultural Symposium).

Greene, W. (2012). *Vegetable gardening the Colonial Williamsburg way: 18th-century methods for today's organic gardener.* Emmaus, PA: Rodale Books.

Harris, J. B. (1989). *Iron pots and wooden spoons: Africa's gifts to New World cooking.* New York: Atheneum.

Hart, J. F. (1991). *The land that feeds us.* New York: W.W. Norton & Co., 277–290.

Hedrick, U. P. (1950). *A history of horticulture in America to 1860.* New York: Oxford University.

Hilliard, S. (1969). Hog meat and cornpone: Food habits in the ante-bellum South. *Proceedings of the American Philosophical Society* 113(1), 1–13.

Kingsolver, B., Hopp, S. J. & Kingsolver, C. (2007). *Animal vegetable miracle: A year of food life.* New York: Harper Perennial.

Levenstein, H. A. (1988). *Revolution at the table: The transformation of the American diet.* New York: Oxford University.

Lewis, E. & Peacock, S. (2003). *The gift of southern cooking.* New York: Alfred Knopf.

Meinig, D. W. (1993). *The shaping of America, V.2: Continental America, 1800–1867.* New Haven, CT: Yale University Press.

Mitchell, P. B. (1993). *Soul on rice: African influences on American cooking.* Chatham, VA: Foodways Publications.

Nathan, J. (June 4, 2003). "Home Cooking: East Meets South at a Delta Table," *New York Times.* F5. http://www.nytimes.com/2003/06/04/dining/home-cooking-east-meets-south-at-a-delta-table.html. Accessed April 11, 2014.

Shortridge, B. G. & Shortridge, J. R. (1995). Cultural geography of American food-ways: An annotated bibliography. *Journal of Cultural Geography,* 15, 79–108.

Southern Living Magazine. (2005). *Best kept secrets of the South's best cooks.* Birmingham, AL: Oxmoor House.

Sylvest, T. A. (2008). *Collard greens: Growing up on a Sandhill subsistence farm in Louisiana during the Great Depression.* Bloomington, IN: Authorhouse.

Tsunoda, S. and Gomez-Campo, C. (1980). *Brassica crops and wild allies.* Tokyo: Japan Scientific Societies Press.

Westmacott, R. (1992). *African American gardens and yards.* Knoxville, TN: University of Tennessee Press.

Wright, R. (1945). *Black boy: A record of childhood and youth.* New York: Harper & Bros.

Zelinsky, W. (2001). *The enigma of ethnicity: Another American dilemma.* Iowa City: University of Iowa Press.

Zohary, D. & Hopf, M. (1993). *Domestication of plants in the Old World: The origin and spread of cultivated plants in West Asia, Europe, and the Nile Valley, Second Edition* (Oxford: Clarendon).

Index